LIGHTING

EXTERIORS & LANDSCAPES

LIGHTING

EXTERIORS & LANDSCAPES

WANDA JANKOWSKI

Architecture & Interior Design Library

An Imprint of
PBC International, Inc.

Distributor to the book trade in the United States and Canada:
Rizzoli International Publications Inc.
300 Park Avenue South
New York, NY 10010

Distributor to the art trade in the United States and Canada:
PBC International, Inc.
One School Street
Glen Cove, NY 11542
1-800-527-2826
Fax 516-676-2738

Distributor throughout the rest of the world:
Hearst Books International
1350 Avenue of the Americas
New York, NY 10019

Library Of Congress Cataloging-in-Publication Data

Jankowski, Wanda
Lighting: exteriors and landscapes / by Wanda P. Jankowski.
     p.   cm.
     Includes index.
     ISBN 0–86636–237–1   (international version: ISBN 086636-298-3)
     1. Exterior lighting. 2. Lighting, Architectural and decorative.
3. Garden lighting   I. Title.
TK4188.J36   1993   93–30528
621.32'29--dc20   CIP

CAVEAT– Information in this text is believed accurate, and will pose
no problem for the student or casual reader. However, the author
was often constrained by information contained in signed release
forms, information that could have been in error or not included at
all. Any misinformation (or lack of information) is the result of failure
in these attestations. The author has done whatever is possible to
insure accuracy.

Color separation, printing and binding by
Dai Nippon Printing Group

Printed in Hong Kong

10 9 8 7 6 5 4 3 2 1

CONTENTS

CHAPTER 1
PUBLIC SPACES

CHAPTER 2
PARKS AND PLAZAS

CHAPTER 3
CORPORATE BUILDINGS

CHAPTER 4
HOSPITALITY AND RETAIL

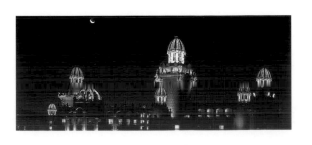

FOREWORD

ABE FEDER, FIES, FIALD
LIGHTING BY FEDER

There's a common confusion about "exterior lighting"—it's too pat a phrase. The key to understanding exterior lighting is to examine what the purpose for outdoor lighting was in the first place. In primitive days, a thousand years ago in Central America, and centuries ago in Greece, they built arenas in stone where they performed their rituals at night. And what did they use to see at night? Fire. Can you imagine five thousand people sitting in an outdoor arena with hundreds of pots of fire aglow? So there were inventive devices used to light the outdoors before history.

Exterior lighting is not new, nor should it be narrowly defined. After all, what is the need for light? Why did past civilizations have outdoor events? Their events took place outside at night because there was a sense of spectacle commonly enjoyed by all people. There ought to be a projection of this philosophy in the exterior lighting of any structure—what is it for? And just as importantly, consider the human reactions and need for light—who is it for?

Most of the time, pure invention never happens in lighting independently of the surrounding circumstances or situations, as it does when some first-of-their-kind goods are created. The invention of a technological development or technique in lighting happens when specific purposes must be fulfilled. In terms of lighting a building, it becomes very simple: invention grows out of a practical need.

The basic existence of exterior lighting equipment, for example, depends on the light source. There would not have been Rockefeller Center exterior lighting, for example, if General Electric Lighting hadn't developed the first 1500-watt multi-vapor lamp that produced 75,000 lumens.

In the future, will there be more light used in the outdoors? Of course, because we're night people, and we will make use of the incredible tools available on our own behalf.

The role of the architect is to encompass all the patterns of the owner, and what the owner wants, and to put the patterns together to create a living environment. Sometimes creation intrudes on this process, and something else that's different evolves from it. The lighting designer's and engineer's role is to see to it that what the architect has done fits together; that it is technically solid and all forces of heat, air and light function within it.

But the wonder of it is that lighting is never really static, because, at any particular moment, who is to say, "These are the limitations; these are the only tools you have," when all of a sudden there can be a breakthrough—practical need pushing creativity and invention—that turns the tool itself into something else. That's why the role of the lighting designer should include an understanding of where the development of the tools is going, especially today, in view of the economics involved in designing, installing and maintaining lighting systems.

When you hear the head of a power authority say an incandescent lamp should not be used anymore—it's a waste of energy and all that—obviously, he isn't informed about the changes that are taking place. Since my youth the incandescent lamp was 90 percent heat; 10 percent light. Who would have dreamt that a coating of IR quartz tube would freeze the heat and create light, and put us now at the threshold of 40 percent light and 60 percent heat. And how soon will it be at 60 and 40, or how soon will it be 80 and 20—and with no transformers, and brilliant color. This tells you one very important thing—the unknown is with us here and now, waiting to be grasped and fathomed.

Light isn't bricks, it isn't steel, it isn't pat. There's an effusiveness in the light material. And I've been privy to that as I've seen it evolve over a period of 50 years. The breakthroughs into the secrets of light are just beginning, and that's an ingredient in designing lighting, for exteriors and interiors, that can't be ignored.

Abe Feder, FIES, FIALD, was the first independent lighting designer in both the theatrical and architectural worlds. His firm, Lighting By Feder, is located in New York City.

His Broadway credits are legion and include My Fair Lady and Camelot. His architectural credits include the United Nations, Philharmonic Hall at Lincoln Center, the terminal plaza of Kennedy International Airport, the Kennedy Center for the Performing Arts in Washington, D.C., and Rockefeller Center in New York: Plaza and Facade, Atlas Sculpture, Prometheus Fountain, the International Building lobby, and the GE Building lobby murals. He is responsible for many bulb and fixture developments which are now catalog standards.

Abe Feder was the first President of the International Association of Lighting Designers (IALD) and is an IALD Fellow, as well as a Fellow of the Illuminating Engineering Society of North America (IESNA).

EXTERIOR LIGHTING IN THE U.S. IN THE NINETIES

WANDA P. JANKOWSKI
Editor-in-Chief
ARCHITECTURAL LIGHTING

Wanda Jankowski is well known to many in the lighting and interior design, and architecture fields. She has been Editor-in-Chief of *Architectural Lighting* magazine since 1989. From 1980 to 1985 she was Editor-in-Chief of *Lighting Design + Application* magazine and the Journal of IES, both publications of the Illuminating Engineering Society of North America (IESNA). Prior to that she held various editorial positions with the Society and served as Staff Coordinator for the International Illumination Design Awards Program.

Ms. Jankowski holds a BA from St. Joseph's College and an MA degree from St. John's University. Ms. Jankowski has published several books with PBC International including *Kitchens and Baths* (1993), *Designing With Light: Residential Interiors* (1991) and *The Best of Lighting Design* (1987). She has authored articles for magazines and newspapers on a variety of subjects, including light, and she is a member of the Authors Guild.

Though the energy crisis caused the outdoors in the United States to go dark in many places, several factors have played into the rebirth and resurgence of interest in outdoor lighting in the past decade, and now, into the 1990s. Perhaps the strongest driving force for the use of exterior lighting is economics. The recessive economy has led building owners and developers to seize the opportunity exterior lighting allows them to make their properties visually more attractive, and in turn, attract tenants. Lighting in combination with architectural details and graphics, can establish a positive, quality image for a commercial corporation or complex.

Safety and security are also considerations that come into play in owners' decisions to light their properties at night. Our mobile society enjoys evening recreation now more than ever— whether it's driving to a shopping mall, or strolling through a public park or plaza. But the public will only come if assured that the environment is safe. Good lighting helps deter loitering, vandalism and crime, and so can help eliminate many safety concerns that have an impact on how successful the use of a public space will be at night.

maintain, because of the image, comfort and safety benefits drawn from them. The development and refinement of dimming and controls has also increased energy savings and can extend lamp life for less efficient sources, like incandescent, that have other advantageous characteristics, so that they don't have to be replaced as frequently.

The trend towards the development of smaller light sources and the accompanying design and manufacture of less bulky fixtures to house them has given lighting professionals more options to create designs that complement architecture and allow the effects of light to be appreciated, while the fixtures remain unobtrusive. Fixtures expertly concealed and positioned in foliage, for example, can eke out a living sculpture of textured, natural landscape elements from what would have been complete one-dimensional darkness without the benefit of illumination.

Decorative fixtures are in abundance today in a variety of styles, and make possible the ability to beautify the environment as well as provide non-glaring, comfortable illumination for pedestrians and motorists. Sconces, whether standard or

© 1993 Robert Eovaldi

In public spaces, lighting can allow pedestrians to feel safe at night. Merchants on Ann Arbor's Main Street have experienced an upswing in retail sales at night since the new lighting system was installed.

Fortunately, most kinds of lighting used in outdoor applications are energy efficient. High-pressure sodium and metal halide lamps, two of the most energy efficient sources available, are popular for use in outdoor lighting systems, and given the above considerations, are perceived as worth the cost and energy to design, install and

custom designed, or decorative and pole-mounted luminaires are offered in a range of contemporary and traditional styles. And the increasing sophistication of lensing and optical reflector systems has eliminated much of the concern for light trespass or pollution.

Exterior lighting can provide a corporate client with a strong visual identity by night. Such is the case with the facade lighting of the Prudential Building.

While the goal of the exterior lighting design may be to enhance the architecture, technical and practical requirements need to be satisfied as well. These include selecting lighting systems which incorporate features such as vandal-resistance, weather- and water-proofing, corrosion resistance, and easy installation.

Ease of maintenance is important as well, because, after all, if a maintenance employee cannot easily reach a fixture to change a burnt-out lamp, the lighting design will be destroyed. And if exotic lamps and fixtures, or systems from unreliable manufacturers are installed, the chances of accessing replacement equipment when components break or wear out are slim and do not bode well for keeping the design intact in the future.

Available lighting accessories, such as color filters, louvers, and computer programming systems, make it possible today to offer the building owner flexibility, so the lighting can be changed to suit varied seasons, holidays or special occasions.

The projects collected in this book demonstrate the fact that there is no one way to light a building, retail or hospitality setting, or a public space or park. One approach is to render the building by night the way it appears in daylight. Another is to create a completely different appearance by night than is viewed during the day. In some applications, color and motion have been added to lend some imagination-expanding pizzazz to the urban landscape.

Techniques used range from floodlighting with broad washes of illumination, to outlining the striking architectural features of a structure with linear light sources, such as neon or fiberoptics. To enhance the beauty of period architecture, decorative fixture treatments that double as functional task lighting units may be installed. In other cases, the clean lines of a modern smooth facade may call for a design approach that conceals the fixtures while only revealing the light effects. And also interesting is the use of light in art and as an artwork in itself. Though outdoor laser performances and light shows are more popular in Europe and Japan, interest in the United States has been growing in recent years.

The key to a quality lighting design is really the contracting of a qualified lighting-related professional who can combine technical expertise with an artistic and creative approach to architectural enhancement. I'm taking this opportunity to thank all the designers and photographers who contributed their outstanding work to this book. Special thanks goes to Motoko Ishii and J.F. Caminada for sharing their thoughts via words and photographs on the state of lighting in Japan and Europe, respectively.

Light can be used to highlight ornate architectural details, while the actual fixtures remain concealed and unobtrusive, seen here in the Palace of Fine Arts.

We tried to present a range of common applications—from corporate facades and plazas, and retail and hospitality, to public parks, structures and works of art. We hope you, the reader, will use this comprehensive collection of commercial outdoor projects and products as a reference, as well as an inspiration and starting point for your own creative designs.

One of the newest light sources available for use in exterior lighting is fiberoptics. The light source is concealed in an illuminator remotely located, so only the durable, non-electric fibers are exposed to climate conditions. Here, lines of fiber illuminate a bridge by night.

EXTERIOR LIGHTING IN EUROPE IN THE NINETIES

J.F. CAMINADA
Editor-in-Chief

INTERNATIONAL LIGHTING REVIEW

Mr. J.F. Caminada was born in
Paris, France, in 1943. He studied
architecture in Paris, and in Delft,
The Netherlands. Since 1971,
he has been with Philips Lighting at
its headquarters in Eindhoven,
The Netherlands, as a staff architect
and lighting designer. He is also
Editor-in-Chief of the quarterly magazine published by Philips Lighting,
the *International Lighting Review*.

Although the post office airmail rate for "Europe" now extends to the Bering Strait, lighting in the (West) European Community will be the subject here. The last decade of the century, and this is perhaps the reason, is a period full of "posts."

Whether you like it or not, there is, or was, something like a postmodern architecture and design. At the same time, we seem to have arrived in a "post-material" era, as a consequence and conclusion of the two preceding ones. The 1950s, dominated in Europe by the reconstruction, was a practical and "traditional" era. The 1960s and early 1970s were a material and "functional" era, aiming at more of the well-earned, post-war prosperity. The sky was the limit, and almost nobody knew that there was, already, a hole in it.

This, at times euphoric, period came to an abrupt end early in the 1970s with the arrival of the oil crisis—often improperly referred to as the energy crisis. A period of recession followed, during which any manifest use of energy, as in lighting, was frowned upon, ignoring the fact that of the 95 percent of the energy used for everything else, much was wasted. This probably marked the start of our present "post-material" era, in which the environment is given a high value, but with more sense for reality than in the 1960s.

Lighting in Europe

The European lighting industry reacted strongly to the shock of the oil crisis with a stream of innovative, if not new, light sources and systems—although these did not reach the market before the early 1980s. Triphosphor (compact) fluorescent lamps date from this period, followed by white high-pressure sodium (HPS). Oddly enough, all were developed for indoor use, but were quickly accepted outdoors.

The evolution of lighting practice saw the same landmarks as mentioned above. A street lighting luminaire, in the 1950s, was basically no more than a metal basin with an incandescent or mercury lamp in it, pouring its light onto lots of bicycles and a few cars.

The 1960s redesigned the basin, added a reflector, a new lamp (HPS), and squeezed every lumen out of it to illuminate lots of cars and a few bicycles. The pedestrian, this "obstacle," had to wait until the 1970s to get his own dedicated streets in city centers. Here ambience and style were considered at least as important as illuminance.

This might be at the root of today's trend toward decorativeness, and our love of the historical in outdoor luminaires *(Fig. 1)*. Period luminaires are even installed where they had never before been seen.

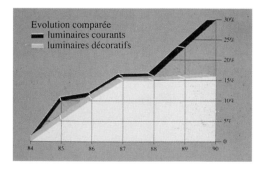

Fig. 1 Lyon, France (inner: 430,000 inhabitants, greater: 1.2 million). The evolution of the number and types of luminaires in the City of Lyon showing the growth of decorative luminaires. Red=standard luminaires. Ochre=decorative luminaires.

A new era had dawned for the public lighting engineer. Until now, he had been almighty in his field, and undisturbed by the architect, who considered lighting as something literally without substance. But then the architect began to take an active interest in lighting, and the public lighting engineer, who felt uneasy in the aesthetics of design, was quite happy with this awakening interest from the architect provided that the newcomer did not try to overrule him in technical matters. And so a truce was signed. But most architects are still more interested in luminaires for their own sake, than that these should produce adequate lighting: beauty AND function.

In the meantime, the public is growing used to the idea that environmental issues can be approached in a realistic and positive way. Energy conservation is here to stay; but better, and even more lighting can go with it. This and city beautification might be today's key words.

Energy Conservation

Since 1960, we have seen the number of light points in major European cities increase by a factor of at least five *(Fig. 2)*. (For example, the city of Paris has 110,000 light points and spends 175,000 USD/day on lighting.) And yet, at the same time, the energy consumed by the lighting has increased only three-fold. This clearly demonstrates two things:

- Energy-saving measures and new sources were successful.
- Using (more) electricity for (more) lighting is accepted as a positive fact.

- ■— *number of light points*
- ●— *luminous flux*
- ×— *electrical power*
- ▼— *efficacy (lumens per watt)*

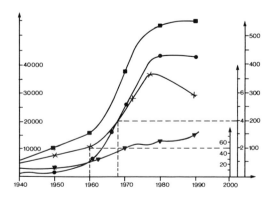

Fig. 2 Malmo, Sweden. Curves showing the development of Malmo (230,000 inhabitants) city lighting. Note decrease of energy with increase in number of light points. Key: number of light points, luminous flux, electrical power, efficacy (lumens per watt).

The stream of innovations from the 1980s is still continuing. The birth of a new light source was seen in 1991 with the electrodeless QL induction lamp system *(Fig. 3)*, in which the gas discharge is brought about with the aid of an induced electromagnetic field. This very same principle of induction was used to check if incandescent lamps had been sufficiently pumped out in the Philips factory in...1891.

The QL's lifetime is rated at 60,000 hours, which means more than 15 years of public lighting without replacement. This innovative feature triggered the creativity of many designers, city architects included *(Figs. 4a, 4b, 4c)*.

Fig. 3 The QL induction lighting system. Each lamp has its own HF generator.

Figs. 4a–4b Helios luminaire in a timeless style designed by the Municipality of Copenhagen for one QL induction lamp system of 85 watts.

Fig. 4c Period luminaire rebuilt for one QL induction lamp system of 85 watts on a world-famous tourist hot-spot: Place du Tertre in Paris.

White high-pressure sodium ("white-SON") was born in 1986 with the color, but not the short lifetime, of incandescents. It quickly found application in those luminaires designed for gas that had later been rebuilt for incandescents *(Fig. 5)*.

Fig. 5 Period luminaires rebuilt for white high-pressure sodium (white SON) 50-watt lamps in old Copenhagen.

New "period" luminaires for white HPS are marketed now, but modern ones have also been designed *(Fig. 6)*. Today, white HPS is entering the field of small-scale floodlighting, so far mainly covered by tungsten halogen.

The excellent color properties of both QL and white-SON is certainly a reason for their increasing application, which underlines the move towards the appreciation of quality in lighting by the public.

Quality in lighting, and energy conservation, are also served by a better optical control of beam and thus the reduction, if not the elimination, of disturbing and wasted spill-light. This was the motivation for the simultaneous development (a novelty) of a new lamp and luminaire. The lamp is a metal halide lamp of 1800 watts with excellent color properties. The luminaire is an extremely compact floodlight system *(Fig. 7)*.

Fig. 6 Contemporary luminaires for white HPS (white SON) 50-watt lamps in The Hague, The Netherlands.

Fig. 7 ArenaVision floodlight system for one metal halide 1800-watt lamp.

Although developed for stadium lighting, this floodlight system, with a maximum intensity of 4.5 million candelas, was quickly discovered for use in the illumination of tall buildings *(Fig. 8)*, and even natural sites *(Figs. 9–10)*.

Fig. 9 (below) and Fig. 10 (next page) Lighting natural monuments. Lighting monuments and sites can be extended to their natural setting. This is what was realized on a large scale at Cuenco, Spain. Not only the village itself was lighted, but also the ravine and mountain behind it by means of 1800-watt ArenaVision floodlights.

Fig. 8 St. Paul's, London, illuminated by the sharply cut-off beams of the ArenaVision system.

City Beautification by Lighting

Floodlighting the church around the corner is no longer seen as an unnecessary use of electricity, as it would have been in the mid-1970s. It adds beauty to the environment which, after all, starts around the corner.

But this new enthusiasm for light must be controlled. This is the reason why, in many European countries, France leading the way, lighting master plans are being formulated. What is a lighting master plan?

A lighting master plan is a definition of the role to be fulfilled by lighting in the city. And it is now not confined to traffic—it is much more ambitious. It starts with a thorough analysis of the city in order to define its present urban and social characteristics and overall "personality."

It aims at:

- improving the nightly ambience and image of the city for visitors and residents
- underlining sites of activity
- increasing the nightly "readability" of the city, both from close up and from far away, by adequately lighting access roads and perspective views and landmarks
- highlighting interesting sites, or mere objects

All this, of course, while respecting the "old" lighting criteria relevant to traffic safety, and today's new ones in Europe concerned with personal safety. It results in a document defining:

- the sites to light in the near future (and those that might best be left shrouded in the darkness of night!)

- light colors
- mounting heights, with regard to the architectural environment

Such a master plan is basically a framework *(Fig. 11)*. A city like Lyon, France's second city, added imaginative initiatives to encourage lighting, namely a kind of partnership between private owners and the city. The owner pays for the illumination study concerning his building, and the cost of the equipment, and the city pays the installation and running costs *(Figs. 12a–12b)*.

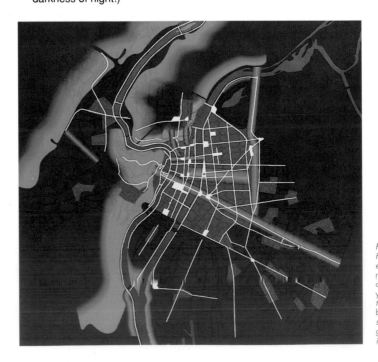

Fig. 11 Lyon's lighting master plan. Headlines of Lyon's city lighting plan to exploit the scenic potential of natural sites: green: with a vegetal character ochre: with an urban character yellow: to improve the "reading" of nocturnal routes and major road axes blue: to create a "light spectacle" emphasizing the major perspectives of the city gray: to emphasize the architectural heritage and picturesque elements of the city.

Figs. 12a–12b Views of the banks of the Rhone, a corner-piece in Lyon's lighting master plan.

Conclusion

Lighting, and especially outdoor lighting, is becoming increasingly popular in Europe today, which is a welcome counterweight to the recession in the building industry affecting indoor lighting. The independent lighting designer is, here, a member of a new, fast-growing profession. There are those, however, who tend to consider it as a purely artistic business, whose boring technical aspects are to be solved by others, such as lighting engineers and equipment manufacturers. And yet outdoor lighting, in European climates, is a serious matter in which technical lighting parameters, sturdiness, safety and maintenance may not be neglected.

If the new European lighting designers are able to adjust their role in order to cooperate harmoniously with the other parties, especially those responsible for public lighting, we might all profit from a most positive "climate" for lighting.

Europe, East and West, has an immense heritage, both man-made and natural, to be lighted or relighted.

Exterior Lighting in Japan in the Nineties

MOTOKO ISHII
President

MOTOKO ISHII LIGHTING DESIGN INC.

A pioneer of lighting design in Japan, Motoko Ishii has received numerous international awards. For her lighting design of the Electric Power Pavilion at the International Garden & Greenery Expo, Osaka 1990, she was named the 1990 recipient of the Edwin F. Guth Memorial Award of Distinction by the IESNA. In 1992, she received three Awards of Merit for Gifu Memorial Center, Hotel New Otani, and Pacifico Yokohama also from the IESNA.

Born in Tokyo, Mrs. Ishii graduated from the Tokyo University of Fine Arts in 1962, was employed as a member of the Design Section of Oy Stockman Orno Ab in Helsinki, Finland, from 1965–66, and of the Design Section of Firma Licht in Raum in Dusseldorf, Germany from 1966–67. In 1968 she established Motoko Ishii Lighting Design Inc. in Tokyo, Japan. Her published works include *Design for Environmental Lighting* (1984), *My World of Lights* (1985), and *Light to Infinity* (1991).

One-half of this earth is always covered by the darkness of night, and night is one-half of each day. Every time I see an image of the earth sent by a space shuttle or satellite, my eyes are captured by the dark half of the earth. Looking out of a plane window or making an overseas telephone call to the United States, Europe or other Asian country never fails to remind me that it is always night for one-half of the earth...and night provides the scene in which a lighting designer can take an active part.

A city at night is a vast black canvas to me, and I use light, rather than paint, to create my images on a grand scale. I consider myself fortunate to live in this era, since there is such a wide variety of light sources available. Needless to say, in creating a design, I must also take into consideration such important factors as energy conservation and coexistence with nature.

I studied lighting design in Finland and West Germany in the late 1960s, and spent the early 1970s in the United States. Since then, I have worked on projects in many cities in Asia, the Middle East, the United States and Australia, but mostly in Japan. In this book, five of my projects in Japan are included, and in this introduction, I will explain how lighting design has developed in this country.

Upon returning to Japan from my lighting design studies in Europe, I began trying to enlighten people regarding the existence and importance of lighting design. At that time, most Japanese people had no idea of what the term "lighting design" meant. We've certainly come a long way since then.

A New Era—The 1980s

Expo '70 Osaka seemed to provide a favorable situation, but soon thereafter Japan found itself suffering from the effects of the first oil crisis, which occurred in early 1970s; energy saving was emphasized and people regarded lighting, even neon signs, with enmity. In the 1980s, after a long period of dormancy, lighting design began to bloom. Why did lighting design begin to come into its own in the 1980s? There were many contributing factors.

First, Japan's improved economic condition. The yen became a strong international currency and Japan earned its place among the world's richest countries. The Japanese had lived poor and frugal lives since the Meiji Era (1868-1912), but have recently achieved a comfortable, high standard of living. In the past, priority was given to industrial development, but now spending money improving their surroundings and creating urban spectaculars can be considered a matter of course for the Japanese. The many years since the oil crisis, which extinguished the lights, have seen the production of a continuing, stable supply of electricity which has helped to increase the demand for lighting.

The second factor is internationalization. Political and economic relations among the nations of the world have become closer. The frequent comings and goings of people have made Tokyo one of the world's most cosmopolitan cities. The city is awake 24 hours a day. Round-the-clock action in cities means that nighttime lighting is of even greater importance.

"Round-the-clock action in cities means that nighttime lighting is of even greater importance," says Mrs. Ishii, who designed gradually changing illumination for the facade of the NEC headquarters building to add interest to the cityscape.

The third factor is an increased interest in culture by the Japanese people. Businesses, previously interested solely in the pursuit of economic benefits, have turned their interest to culture. This has resulted in the emergence of the concept "enterprise culture," an idea never considered in the 1970s. Design has also become more important for cultural promotion. Up-to-date companies know more about the importance of design. Thus, lighting design has gained recognition as an effective means of creating a visual concept.

For my part, these circumstances have given me more opportunities to travel abroad, and I've been deeply impressed by what I've seen around the globe. The aurora I saw from the air over Siberia on my way home from Paris was like a vast screen seen through the airplane window, varying momentarily in color and shape of light, and covering a huge expanse. The full moon at night above thick, white clouds viewed from the airplane on the way home from Guam—the most beautiful, cleanest possible moonlight. The long-lasting glow of sunset seen from the airplane on my way to Los Angeles; the brightness of which, like a rainbow framed by white clouds and the deep blue sky, turned into the glow of morning all too soon, without ever becoming night. The white clouds spreading over the sky, a scene

The increased interest in culture by the Japanese people has led to a greater demand for expression of it through all aspects of design. A sacred ceremony at the Shiga Sacred Garden included a laser light performance designed by Mrs. Ishii.

which never bores me—elegant, silky clouds, dynamic columns of clouds, wonderful cap clouds....that the globe is round is an easily proven truth; this increases my happiness about being alive in the latter half of the twentieth century. At the same time, it reminds me of the plain fact that the night is a half of one day.

Cities and Environments in Harmony

For a long time, man "lived" only during the daylight hours. Civilization and culture were created mostly during the daylight hours. Colors, shapes, products, styles of living; most of the elements comprising human culture were initially carried out during daylight. In my lighting designs, I endeavor to create new spaces within the 12 nighttime hours by using electric energy and combining the hundreds of thousands of available light sources with state-of-the-art technology. There are few spaces left to develop.

What I am trying to do is different from imitating sunlight. I am not trying to invent a source of light similar to solar light or turn night into day, a goal for which many lighting technologists have striven in the past. Night and day are different. The earth and its creatures know that. I believe the lighting designer's target is the use of light at night unlike that in daytime and the creation of new lighting environments different from those during daylight.

I would like to create a total lighting environment which will result in harmony between the city and its environmental lighting. We have carried out the lighting up of huge structures such as towers and bridges. I have also had the opportunity to realize a long-cherished dream to light up historical buildings and natural scenery in various locations. Unfortunately, however, these are just small dots in the overall scale of cities.

Yoichi Yamazaki

A trademark of Mrs. Ishii's designs is the use of state-of-the-art technology and techniques, as found, for example, in the ground-inset LEDs for the Minato Mirai project in Grand Mall Park.

Yoichi Yamazaki

Mrs. Ishii seeks to "create a total lighting environment which will result in harmony between the city and its environmental lighting." The Yokohama Bridge lighting draws visual bonds among the bridge, the city surrounding it, and the moving waters below it.

Lighting design has to be planned and carried out for the city as a whole. Individual lights glittering here and there cannot make a beautiful overall scene. The creation of a harmonious lighting environment is important.

Compatibility of natural and artificial light is also important. It is discouraging that to the camera "eyes" of a satellite, the advanced nations of the world appear to be covered with lights. This means that light which should be shining for us on earth is being diffused wastefully in the air.

Human beings have always loved moonlight and starlight. Even in a modern city, people should be able to enjoy natural light in comfortable coexistence with artificial light.

Moloko Ishii Lighting Design Inc.

Music and light combined to produce an outdoor entertainment event at the Gifu Memorial Center that reflects Mrs. Ishii's philosophy "to create a richer and more beautiful environment" with light.

Baltazair Korab

In recent years, light shows have become a popular and exciting way to celebrate special occasions. This laser art performance in front of Vienna's Rathaus, designed by Mrs. Ishii, commemorated the 120th anniversary of Austro-Japanese friendship.

The problems of energy and comfort are also important topics. Artificial light owes its life to electric energy. The specter of an energy shortage in any country looms in the future, perhaps even sooner than we realize. For this reason, we must strive to save energy.

Lighting accounts for about 14 percent of all the electricity used in Japan and Europe. This figure represents only about four percent of the overall demand for energy. But, while energy is limited and must be used accordingly, it is also important to use light as an amenity to create a richer and more beautiful environment. On the other hand, what type of lighting environment best suits human beings must also be considered.

The industrial age saw a continuing increase in the intensity of illumination in the working environment in an effort to obtain increased production. It was thought that intensities as high as thousands of lux would provide a good working environment. I feel that a really comfortable level of illumination for daily life would be found in a lower intensity range. Even a specialist can't tell the difference between 800 and 1000 lux with the naked eye. The difference between 50 and 100 lux can, however, be detected easily by the average person; the difference between 1 and 10 lux can be detected with even greater accuracy. Within the range between 0.1 (the brightness of a full moon at night) and 100 lux, the sensitivity of the human eye seems to narrow arithmetically as the intensity of light increases. Quality lighting at lower levels can best be enjoyed when the brightness and darkness levels are in harmony. This is important for both indoor and outdoor spaces.

BLIC SPACES

The goals of public space lighting are varied, and often one lighting design must satisfy not only aesthetic requirements, but provide for vandal-resistance, durability and easy maintenance. Included in this chapter are installations which have been renovated, and as part of the rich transformations, existing lighting which had rendered the facades dull and flat have been replaced with ones in which the intricate architectural details are emphasized with depth and dimension. Other refurbished landmark buildings have had illumination added for the first time. These installations span the country—Michigan State Capitol, New York City's Grand Central Terminal, National Cathedral in Washington, D.C., and the Palace of Fine Arts in San Francisco—and each is illuminated using a rationale that developed to suit the particular circumstances of the project.

Since public facilities are usually built to last decades, the architecture and integral lighting often must possess a timeless quality, so that the building does not appear dated over time. The Orange County and Broward County Convention Centers have had lighting designed with this consideration a primary criterion.

Light can enliven a public space, and add a touch of excitement to the environment. Grandel Square, via pattern projections, bursts of grazing light and lines of fiberoptics, is a visual nighttime fantasy that extends the theatrical experience enjoyed by area theatergoers to the outdoors.

Yokohama Bay Bridge, through the use of filtered light, has become a colorful time signal for passing motorists. And colored lighting and furnishings are used to create a healing atmosphere for patients and visitors at Health Central medical facility.

Of course, function and safety are also primary concerns in designing lighting for public spaces. St. Louis Union Station lighting succeeds in creating a comfortable and safe, as well as an aesthetically striking atmosphere for those visiting the complex. And the relighting of Ann Arbor's Main Street has brought smiles to the boulevard's merchants, who have noticed that along with better lighting and a greater feeling of safety and security has come an increase in nighttime shoppers.

Energy saving is an important environmental issue in the 1990s and will continue to be beyond this decade. So it is refreshing to see that an energy-efficient lighting design, such as that for the Minnesota Department of Revenue, can be attractive and complementary to the building architecture as well.

PALACE OF FINE ARTS

CRITERIA

To commemorate the completion of the Panama Canal, and in celebration of the rebirth of San Francisco after the great earthquake, the Palace of Fine Arts was designed by architect Bernard Maybeck and built for the Pan-Pacific International Exposition of 1915.

Over time, the structure deteriorated, and in 1967, a concrete reconstruction was completed, today a historic landmark situated on the western edge of the San Francisco Marina District.

The Palace is actually a terra-cotta-colored, 130-foot-tall, open-air central rotunda, adorned with eight sculpture panels and eight statues, and set before a 70-foot-tall colonnade.

The Palace had been lit in the late 1960s, backlighted with 60 1000-watt incandescent fixtures, a scheme long outdated and in need of redesign. Because the structure is a historic landmark, the lighting designer, Ross De Alessi, had to conduct extensive historical research and obtain civic approvals before the new lighting could be designed. Other requirements of the design included vandal resistance, an energy draw limited to 60 kilowatts, stringent construction budgets, and the complete concealment of the fixtures during the day.

Project: **Palace of Fine Arts**   Location: **San Francisco, California**
Owner: **Recreation and Park Commission, San Francisco**
Architect: **Bernard Maybeck (1861-1957)**
Lighting Designer: **Ross De Alessi, with Luminae Souter Lighting**
Design at the time the lighting was designed; currently with
Ross De Alessi Lighting Design
Engineer & Contractor: **Sasco/Valley Electric**
Photographer: © 1990 Douglas A. Salin
Lighting Manufacturers: **General Electric Lighting, Sterner-Infranor, Columbia, Western Lighting Industries, Stonco, Universal**

FULFILLMENT

To obtain approvals from the Recreation and Park Commission (the owner), the Arts Commission, two neighborhood associations, and the Landmarks Preservation Advisory Board, a rendering of the proposed system, and an on-site mock-up of the effects to be achieved were conducted by the lighting team.

Ross De Alessi specified low-profile and glare-free fixtures in the new lighting design not only to allow the aesthetic beauty of the structure to reign supreme unimpeded by visible units, but to eliminate light trespass which might disturb residents of the Pacific Heights area immediately south of the Palace.

The asymmetric floodlights that footlight the rotunda and colonnade house 150-watt and 250-watt deluxe HPS lamps, and are concealed in concrete vaults topped with metal grates that lock. Some grates have blackout panels welded in place with crossbars removed to allow an even wash of light to be cast out. The fixtures are low profile due to remote ballasting.

The sculpture panels, statuary and rotunda arches are illuminated with low-profile, remote-ballasted asymmetric sign lighters, fitted with high-output tri-phosphor fluorescent lamps. To highlight the *Weeping Maidens* panels, customized, very low-profile, T8 tri-phosphor fluorescent sign lighters are positioned on top of the colonnade on extremely narrow ledges. All fluorescent fixtures have louvers and custom-colored lenses to complement the warm color of the deluxe high-pressure sodium, which, in turn complements the earthy terra-cotta tones of the structure.

The rotunda columns are backlit with crisp, white light from enclosed PAR 38 fixtures, with 250-watt quartz spot lamps in metal plate boxes with locking grates. The *Priestesses of Culture* sculptures inside the rotunda are bathed in focal light from enclosed PAR 56 fixtures with 12-volt PAR 56 lamps, and fitted with custom hoods for glare control. All quartz and incandescent lamps are dimmed 15 percent to extend lamp life.

Three low-profile, custom-colored concrete enclosures contain pier uplights at the 16-foot level.

All fixtures and enclosures have stainless steel tamper-proof hardware. The fixtures are custom painted to protect against corrosion from the marine environment. A private endowment insures that the cleaning and maintenance schedule, including group relamping before end of lamp and color life, is kept up.

The new lighting system illuminates the structures and entire site with a draw of only 44 kilowatts. The entire Palace is lit daily from dusk to 11:30 P.M., with security lighting on walkways and rotunda columns on until daybreak.

Sculpture panels and rotunda arches are lit with remote-ballasted asymmetric sign lighters with tri-phosphor fluorescent lamps.

Fluorescent sign lighters placed on very narrow ledges are fitted with filters so that the light cast matches that of the warm high-pressure sodium fixtures used elsewhere.

The asymmetric floodlights that footlight the colonnade and rotunda contain 150-watt and 250-watt deluxe high-pressure sodium lamps.

Focal light on the *Priestesses of Culture* sculptures inside the rotunda comes from enclosed PAR 56 fixtures fitted with custom hoods for glare control.

Low-profile, glare-free fixtures eliminated light trespass which might have disturbed nearby Pacific Heights area residents.

A high priority was concealing all fixtures so that the architecture could be appreciated unimpeded during the day.

The Palace of Fine Arts is a terra-cotta-colored, 130-foot-tall, open rotunda set before a 70-foot-tall colonnade.

30TH STREET STATION

CRITERIA

The 60-year-old station was due for rehabilitation, and along with interior refurbishing came a new nighttime exterior image. The lighting has been designed to represent what the original building architects might have executed had the technology been available at the time.

The 30th Street Station by day.

FULFILLMENT

To light the facade, a dual-purpose luminaire has been created. Pedestrian-scale poles are equipped with a pair of arms that hold metal halide downlights housed in white half-globes. These fixtures illuminate the sidewalks surrounding the station.

On the top of each pole, mounted above the half-globes, are two 400-watt metal halide floodlights. These floodlights are fitted with pink glass filters, and wash the sides and upper regions of the building. The sides of window niches are illuminated with unfiltered 150-watt metal halide floodlights also mounted on poles above the half-globes. The variation in the color of the light adds a subtle sense of depth and dimension to the formally structured facade.

The exterior lighting fixtures not only successfully enhance the architecture, but bring a balanced sense of aesthetics, comfort and safety through light to the thousands of travelers that use this Philadelphia landmark each year.

Station entrance by day.

Project: **30th Street Station**　　　Location: **Philadelphia, Pennsylvania**　　　Client: **30th Street Limited, L.P. and Amtrak**
Architect: **Dan Peter Kopple, principal, Sherman Aronson, project manager; Dan Peter Kopple & Associates**
Lighting Designer: **Alfred Borden IV,** formerly of the **Kling Lindquist Partnership** and currently with the **Lighting Practice,** and **Kenneth Yarnell, The Kling Lindquist Partnership**
Engineer *(mechanical, electrical, structural and HVAC):* **The Kling Lindquist Partnership**　　　Contractor: **The George Hyman Construction Company**
Photographer: **Robert Golding, B & H Photographics**
Lighting Manufacturers: **Sterner Lighting Systems, Inc.** *(exterior),* **Peerless Lighting** *(interior),* **Central Brass Works** *(interior fixture restoration)*

The luminaires contain a downlighting component that illuminates walkways, and floodlights that uplight the facade.

Incredible throw from the pedestrian-scale, dual-purpose luminaires allows the architecture to be enjoyed unimpeded by overly tall or bulky fixtures.

HEALTH CENTRAL

CRITERIA

Fortunately for patients and visitors, Orlando's Health Central is not a typical, drably colored facility. The bold facade, as well as the interior furnishings, incorporate healing and enlivening colors intended to create an environment that is soothing and, at the same time, hope-filled. Energy-efficient lighting had to be designed by Craig Roeder to extend this philosophy.

FULFILLMENT

This project reflects a not-so-uncommon trend in exterior lighting today. That is, creating an exterior nighttime image for a building via interior illumination visible through expanses of glass curtain walls. The bold red cladding of a portion of the exterior facade is visually juxtaposed with the interior's swirls of "voltarc purple" ceiling-mounted neon visible through the glass.

The exterior image is bolstered as well by a range of 100-watt metal halide fixtures. These include metal halide fixtures that furnish both uplight and downlight in the space-frame canopied entrance area. The uplight shines illumination onto the tubular space-frame structure, and the downlight component allows for a well-lit walkway. Each of the palm trees is grazed by illumination from burial uplights.

The space-frame canopy is lit with metal halide fixtures that have an up/downlight component.

Project: **Health Central**   Location: **Orlando, Florida**   Client: **West Orange Health Care District**   Architect: **Noel Barrick and Johnathan Bailey, AKS Architects**
Landscape Architect: **Fred Halback, Herbert Halback, Inc.**   Lighting Designer: **Craig A. Roeder Associates, Inc.**   Contractor: **Robins Corporation**
Photographer: © **1993 Michael Lowry Photography**   Lighting Manufacturers: **Neotek, Edison Price Lighting, Litelab, Hydrel**

The neon was chosen to complement the vibrant interior furnishings.

Part of the exterior image comes from the interior neon and metal halide lighting visible through the glass curtain walls.

The setting sun produces a golden glow on the bronze reflective glass cladding of the building.

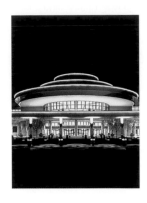

CRITERIA

To complement the distinguished structure designed by Hellmuth, Obata & Kassabaum, Inc. to be the Orange County Convention Center, the client wanted lighting that would not only set it off, but withstand the test of time, and years later remain fresh and undated in the eyes of visitors.

Also, the land between the building site and a main thoroughfare is a protected wetlands area that shelters nocturnal animals. The amount of light trespass permitted was regulated by the Florida Land Management Department.

FULFILLMENT

Respectful of the wetlands area, lighting designer Randy Burkett, Randy Burkett Lighting Design, Inc., opted for shorter pole-mounted, optically precise luminaires on the roadway spaced close together rather than fewer, but taller and more obtrusive high-mast fixtures. Particular light sensitive zones are protected from light trespass through the use of bollards and sharp cutoff uplights.

The building site is demarcated at night with a band of light at the top edge of the retaining wall bordering the lake. The band is created with a strip of 2-watt, low-voltage, subminiature lamps spaced closely together. The lamps are enclosed in a polycarbonate tube that is pressed into a metal extrusion concealed in the wall, and are operated under rated voltage to extend lamp life.

Two low-voltage, submersible pool fixtures fitted with PAR 64 lamps illuminate each of the five water jets in the lake.

The building itself is designed with a minimum of ornamentation, drawing its aesthetic inspiration instead from rounded and balanced shapes and proportions. Consequently, lighting designer Randy Burkett, Randy Burkett Lighting Design, Inc., chose to incorporate primarily indirect lighting inside and out into the architectural elements—parapet walls, balconies and column capitals.

The spaceship-like top of the building is outlined with phosphor-coated luminous tubing that is filled with argon and mercury gases. The tubing is concealed in a recess in the precast concrete parapet wall. After experimenting with mock-ups, the designer selected phosphor-coated tube because of the good, white, slightly warm color and softer glow achieved via the coating.

High-color rendering metal halide fixtures, concealed in planters outside the windows on the second level concourse, light the circular overhang above the second floor. To avoid glare in eyes of building occupants and reflections of the fixtures in windows, the luminaires are located next to windows and aimed outward toward the overhang.

Quarter-round metal halide sconces with narrow distribution reflectors light the underside of the porte cochere and direct illumination in front of columns.

The landscaping around the edges of the building is treated with care. Medium-height trees are uplit with wide-distribution, low-voltage PAR 56 lamps in burial fixtures. Tall palm trees are lighted with the same fixture, but with narrow-distribution lamps that graze the trunks and highlight the undersides of the foliage.

Project: **Orange County Convention and Civic Center**
Location: **Orange County, Florida**
Client: **Orange County**   Architect: **Hellmuth, Obata, & Kassabaum, Inc.,
Tampa and VOA, Orlando**
Landscape Architect: **Hellmuth, Obata & Kassabaum, Inc., Tampa**
Lighting Designer: **Randy Burkett, Randy Burkett Lighting Design, Inc.**
Photographer: **George Cott, Chroma Inc.**   Engineer: **Sverdrup**
Lighting Manufacturers: **Sterner Lighting, Heath Corporation, General Electric,
Roberts Steplite, Greenlee, Hydrel**

*The client wanted the lighting to be "undated,"
and to remain timeless for years to come.*

Each of the water jets is illuminated with two low-voltage submersible PAR 64 pool fixtures.

Landscaping surrounding the facility is uplit to highlight the plantings and not the luminaires, a concept in keeping with the lighting of the interior and exterior of the building.

The circular top of the building is ringed with phosphor-coated luminous tubing filled with argon and mercury gases.

The indirect lighting elements are an integral part of the building's restrained ornamentation.

MICHIGAN STATE CAPITOL

CRITERIA

The existing illumination had included mercury vapor site and facade lighting systems that made the building appear very green/blue and flat, obscuring the ornate architectural detailing, and producing glare. "There were 1000- and 1500-watt mercury vapor floodlights on the roof of the Capitol, as well as on the roofs of surrounding buildings. If you happened to be walking along the site at night, your eyes were blasted by the huge floodlights," says Gary Steffy, Gary Steffy Lighting Design, whose firm was called in by Quinn Evans Architects to do the relighting at a preset budget.

Layers of light from metal halides correspond to the architecturally distinct levels of the building.

FULFILLMENT

The dome of the Capitol is bathed in layers of light that correspond to its architecturally distinct levels. At the base of the dome, the colonnade is visually silhouetted by uplight from adjustable fixtures lamped with 100-watt 3200 degree Kelvin clear metal halides and set behind each column.

On the next level, where the windows are shorter, one adjustable fixture, lamped also with a 100-watt 3200 degree Kelvin metal halide, has been aimed straight up in front of each window to illuminate that 12-foot portion of the dome.

The rounded top of the dome is lit with roof-mounted 100-watt metal halide spotlights. Larger-size units, designed specifically to produce a long throw of light that projects more than a million candlepower center beam with a 100-watt metal halide lamp, illuminate the lantern and spire. Fluorescent striplights have also been mounted inside the lantern to create the impression of a glow emanating from within.

Facade lighting is accomplished with 100-watt metal halide flood-lights set on three-inch concrete pads, and positioned approximately 10 feet out from the facade all the way around the perimeter of the building. The pediments are washed with soft light cast from 100-watt spotlights mounted in a pit in the ground.

At the building entry, asymmetric fixtures wash the ceiling of the porch. The incandescent pole-mounted fixtures at the entrance are replicas of originals designed as gas lanterns by the original building architect, Roger Meyers, in 1879. Though the originals had been taken down and destroyed, Steffy says, "We had enough photographs from that period of time to be able to replicate them." The new lanterns have etched, seeded, acrylic panels that create a look reminiscent of glass. The etching also obscures the light sources inside—clear traffic signal lamps chosen to create the yellowish aura of a carbon filament.

Single-headed, pole-mounted fixtures that mimic the design of the lanterns are used along the entry pathway.

"With all of that we're using 33 percent less energy than they were using with the old mercury vapor system," says Steffy. "Even with the incandescent pathway lights, because of the efficiency of the metal halide lamps and fixtures, a great deal can be accomplished without using a whole lot of watts."

Project: **Michigan State Capitol**   Location: **Lansing, Michigan**
Architect: **Quinn Evans Architects**
Landscape Architect: **William J. Johnson Associates Inc.**
Lighting Designer: **Gary Steffy Lighting Design Inc.**
Contractor: **The Christman Company**   Photographer: © **1993 Fred Golden**
Lighting Manufacturers: **Washington University Technology Associates, Western Lighting Standards, OSRAM/Sylvania, Peerless Lighting, Sterner Lighting, ARC Sales, Metalux**

The new metal halide and incandescent systems use 33 percent less energy than the old mercury system, and have eliminated glare and revealed the ornate architectural detailing of the building facade and dome.

YOKOHAMA BAY BRIDGE

CRITERIA

The Yokohama Bay Bridge spans the entrance to Yokohama Bay between Honmoku and Daikoku Piers. Its main tower height of 172 meters, and the suspended roadway length of 860 meters make it one of the world's largest cable-suspension bridges.

As part of an event that included "Minato Mirai 21," celebrating the special character of the city of Yokohama and its plans for the future, the Yokohama Bay Bridge was illuminated as an important city landmark.

The specific goals of lighting designer, Motoko Ishii, were to use illumination to enhance the grand scale and dramatize the splendor of the bridge by selecting and emphasizing its particular distinguishing features to create a special, permanent nighttime presence.

FULFILLMENT

To dramatize the height of the white main tower, metal halide lamps have been focused on it. At a counterpoint to this, mercury lamps are positioned at the foot of the tower and focused to enhance the reflection of the bridge in the water.

In addition to overall floodlighting, the tops of main towers are bathed in blue light created by metal halide lamps fitted with colored filters, and xenon lamps. "One of my goals is to express the passage of time in my lighting designs," says Mrs. Ishii. And so, she has created a time signal with light: the blue lighting is turned on 15 minutes before the hour and off on the hour—the changing color of the bridge enhancing the shining sea beneath it.

On-site experiments were conducted to establish the exact color of the lighting. "We also asked the related agencies, Tokyo Metropolitan Expressway Public Corporation and Yokohama City, for their suggestions," says Ishii. "Clear blue is a difficult color to create, but with the cooperation of my technical staff, a new blue filter was developed and we succeeded in producing a clear blue."

The bridge was turned on in Fall 1989, during the time the Yokohama Exotic Showcase event was held, and continues to grow in popularity with local residents and visitors.

Project: **Yokohama Bay Bridge**   Location: **Yokohama, Kanagawa, Japan**   Client: **Metropolitan Public Expressway Corporation, Yokohama**
Lighting Designer: **Motoko Ishii, Motoko Ishii Lighting Design Inc.**   Photographer: **Yoichi Yamazaki**

The tops of the main towers are illuminated with blue filtered light.

View of the Yokohama Bay Bridge from
Yamashita Park.

ST. LOUIS UNION STATION

CRITERIA

Anchoring the south edge, St. Louis Union Station is a 60,000 square foot, $20 million complex that contains two office buildings, a restaurant, and a ten-screen movie theater organized around a public plaza.

The site had been home to a coal-burning power plant built in 1904. In fact, though the four-story office structure, known as the Power House, is reminiscent of the station's old power house, it is a modern-day replacement. A true remnant of the past, however, is the adjacent smokestack, which had been a part of the original plant.

Mackey Mitchell Associates was charged with lighting the towering landmark, which has a circular flue measuring 165 feet high, and a 35-foot-high, 18-square-foot base. The specified lighting system had to be economical to install and operate, and the support brackets had to be designed to complement the "Industrial Romanesque" style and warm, earthy coloring of the structure.

Over the several-year development of the St. Louis Union Station property, Mackey Mitchell Associates was also later charged with lighting the exterior and interior of the Union Station Cinema. What makes this movie theater particularly unusual is that it is situated underneath a major interstate highway on a formerly unused site, the value of which rose when the office and entertainment complex reopened. Building restrictions included easements reserved by the Missouri Highway Department so that the overpass structure would remain available for inspection and maintenance. The large, concrete bridge piers of the highway overpass had to remain in place as well. The lighting design for the theater had to create a welcoming image and make it an attractive destination for moviegoers.

FULFILLMENT

The designers chose to uplight the smokestack with 1,000-watt high-pressure sodium (HPS) fixtures because the warm, yellowish glow of that light source complements the golden color of the smokestack. Using computer modelling techniques, fixture placement was determined to be at best at 8 feet away from the surface of the smokestack. This created a pleasing gradation of light from 170 footcandles at the base to two footcandles at the crown. The fixtures are supported by triangular steel brackets.

The time frame from design to installation of the lighting was only six months. The total installation costs were $25,370, and the energy usage with HPS, one of the most efficient sources, is about 35,200 kilowatts per year.

The facade of the Union Station Cinema is washed by fluorescent fixtures mounted along the top of the building. The lobby illumination, seen through an extensive glass wall above the entrance, creates an attention-getting bank of light. Red-accented bollards lamped with 150-watt A 21 incandescents illuminate the landscaped areas in the public plaza in front of the cinema. Low-voltage strip lights have been recessed into the sidewalk bordering the planting beds.

The cinema building pays homage to the area's past use as a railway site by incorporating a modern-day version of Union Station's steel butterfly-shaped shed in the entrance canopy. The canopy is enlivened with clear incandescent lamps installed along its perimeter at 6 inches on center. Indirect, warm white fluorescent fixtures uplight the creased plaster ceiling in the entry foyer.

Both the smokestack and cinema projects have received Edwin F. Guth Memorial Awards of Merit in the International Illumination Design Awards Program of the Illuminating Engineering Society of North America.

Project: **St. Louis Union Station**   Location: **St. Louis, Missouri**   Client: **Balke Properties, Inc.**   Architect, Landscape Architect & Lighting Designer: **Mackey Mitchell Associates**
Lighting Designer *(also for smokestack)*: **Ward, Rafferty, Jacbos**   Contractor: **Corte Construction Company**   Photographer: **Sam Fentress/Mackey Mitchell Associates**
Lighting Manufacturers: **Erection Materials Engineering Inc.** *(smokestack brackets)*, **Andover Controls, Sentinel Lighting, BEGA, Roberts Step-Lite Systems, Halo** *(interior)*,
H.E. Williams *(interior)*

The yellow glow of high-pressure sodium complements the earth tones of the smokestack and the adjacent brick buildings.

The new buildings are modern interpretations of the industrial vernacular of the area. The site of the complex was once an abandoned rail yard.

Lobby illumination, seen through the glass facade of Union Station Cinema, draws moviegoers to the theater's unusual location beneath an interstate highway.

BROWARD COUNTY CONVENTION CENTER

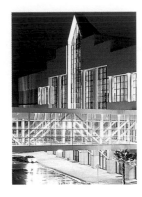

CRITERIA

Since the new facility functions both as a convention and a civic center, and is used frequently for evening functions, the building required a nighttime presence. Also, the structure is not located in the downtown district, but instead is in the wharf area of Fort Lauderdale and is reached by traveling through a working industrial shipyard area or from a bridge on the other side. The client requested the illumination contribute a sense of arrival and anticipation, and add to an atmosphere of quality and safety, whether visitors are arriving for a political rally or special dinner event.

As with most long-term use public facilities, the architecture and lighting had to embody a sense of timelessness, so it would not seem dated and old-fashioned a decade down the road. This philosophy influenced the lighting goals in the sense that a functional, aesthetically pleasing, but discreet design was desired.

FULFILLMENT

Strong exterior lighting is used to reinforce the sense of arrival. The textured columns are grazed with 24-volt, PAR 56 fixtures that are concealed burial units where possible. On upper tiers the fixtures are surface-mounted on the fronts of columns and painted to be as discreet as possible.

As in most convention centers, repetitive structural elements are used like columns and ceiling modules. The grid is broken in the major entry area, which is marked by a vertical, pyramidal-shaped truss. Here very narrow focus metal halide lamps are used for an intentional change in color to visually cue visitors that it is the entrance. The fixtures are mounted in the canopy and uplight the structure which is painted white inside.

Four area lights, not specified by the lighting consultant, light the lower roof area visible in the photo. Though this roof level is not accessible to the general public, it is used occasionally for special functions.

The pole-mounted driveway luminaires are relatively low and unobtrusive, to de-emphasize the utilitarian nature of the drive, and focus the guests' attention on the facade and entrance.

Overall, the lighting is well-integrated with the architecture. The stepped facade at the entrance is emphasized by the distinctive lighting of the pyramidal peak, and the large areas of window walls illuminated from within are complemented by the more gentle grazing of the exterior facade by the sconces and burial uplights. The lighting achieves visual unity with the building structure, while imbuing the environment with a sense of sparkle and excitement.

Project: **Greater Fort Lauderdale/Broward County Convention Center**   Location: **Fort Lauderdale, Florida**   Client: **North Port Venture Association**   Architect: **Cannon**
Landscape Architect: **The SWA Group**   Lighting Designer: **Randy Burkett Lighting Design, Inc.**   Contractor: **Frank J. Rooney, Inc.**   Photographer: **Photo courtesy of Bronzelite.**
Lighting Manufacturers: **Bronzelite, Sterner Lighting**

*Textured columns are grazed with PAR 56
fixtures to emphasize the facade, and
understate the utilitarian aspect of the driveway.*

NATIONAL CATHEDRAL

CRITERIA

The National Cathedral in Washington, D.C. is the second-largest Gothic-style structure in North America. The structure, which took 85 years to construct, was planned originally by George Fredrich Bodley and Henry Vaughan. In 1907, the firm of Frohman, Robb & Little carried on the process, until it was completed under the direction of surviving partner, Philip Hubert Frohman.

The cathedral had been illuminated previously with a wash of color-uncorrected light from metal halide fixtures that rendered the structure flat and lifeless.

The now-retired Canon Clerk of the Works, Richard T. Feller, who represented the Episcopal Bishop, sought to improve the lighting. The funding for the relighting of the facade and west entrance only was made possible by an anonymous donation in honor of the building's completion after the 85-year long construction process.

The cathedral's owners requested that the new lighting design create a dramatic presence for the ornate facade with light sources that remain as unobtrusive and unrevealed as possible, be easy to maintain, and consume low-energy. Remote lighting was also prohibited. A budget was available of $125,000, which not only included equipment and fees, but labor costs to drill into the stonework to conceal wiring.

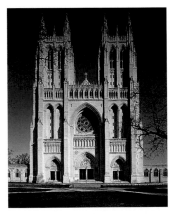

Daytime view of the National Cathedral that took 85 years to build.

FULFILLMENT

Light source options considered and rejected included high-pressure sodium lamps, which would cast the building in too yellow a glow; and color-corrected metal halide lamps, which would bathe it in too cold a light as well as be difficult to color stabilize and dim.

Consequently, three types of incandescent sources were used: PAR 56, 120-watt very narrow spots; 90-watt PAR/FL/H: and 150-watt quartz PAR 38 floods. Most of the 121 lamps are housed in standard can-on-stem fixtures. To achieve a subtle effect, all the fixtures are dimmed a minimum of 50 percent. The dimming also conserves energy and extends lamp life, allowing lamp replacement to be scheduled in two-year cycles.

A mock-up to test fixture locations insured effective placement. Most fixtures are easily accessed without the help of ladders. The facade at the lower portion of the building is lit with flush-mounted uplights concealed below grade at the base of the building. The fixtures flanking the 15-foot-high main doors have been recessed into the stonework. Since remote lighting could not be used, the towers have been illuminated using fixtures mounted behind the parapets.

The fact that the exterior facade isn't broadly washed, but instead columns and archways are highlighted creates a delicate sense of depth and soaring verticality. The facade's nighttime beauty is further enhanced by the interior backlighting of the 60-foot diameter rose window and the viewing gallery above it, timed to be turned on with the exterior lighting.

The nighttime illumination, which is kept on for about five hours per night, costs approximately $1,043 annually (at 7.63 kilowatts per hour).

Since the Cathedral is situated on the highest point in the Capitol, the new lighting is appreciated by many because it is visible for miles. A fund-raising campaign is under way so that the remainder of the structure, which is still illuminated with the original metal halide washes, can be relit to complement the west entrance.

This project received an Award of Excellence in the 1991 GE Lighting Edison Award competition.

Project: **National Cathedral**   Location: **Washington, D.C.**
Owner: **National Cathedral**
Lighting Designer: **Candace M. Kling, Michael Janicek, Peter A Hugh, C.M. Kling and Associates, Inc.**
Electrical Engineer: **Leach Wallace Associates, Inc.**
Electrical Contractor: **Primo Electric Contracting**
Photographer: **James D'Addio**
Lighting Manufacturers: **BEGA**—*fixtures,* **General Electric Lighting**—*lamps*

The restriction that there could be no remote illumination led to the incorporation of lighting fixtures into the stonework at the entrance and behind the parapets.

The upper portions of the facade are lit with dimmed incandescent fixtures hidden behind the balconies.

Daytime view of the unobtrusive fixtures. The facade had previously been bathed in an uncomplimentary cold bluish wash from metal halide fixtures.

The intentionally uneven illumination gives depth and dimension to the ornate architecture.

GRANDEL SQUARE

CRITERIA

The St. Louis entertainment district, which had centered around a group of vaudeville and movie houses, had been subject to deterioration until it finally closed down in the 1960s. Fortunately, the neighborhood has experienced a rebirth, known as the Grand Center cultural district renovation. The newest addition to that cultural district is the Grandel Square Theatre.

Since evening performances are a staple of the theater area, nighttime illumination to provide patrons with a sense of excitement, as well as comfort and safety was important.

Lighting designers Randy Burkett and Katherine Abernathy from Randy Burkett Lighting Design in St. Louis, worked in collaboration with New York-based Broadway freelancer Peter Kaczorowski to incorporate into the lighting project an adjacent sculpture, an abandoned movie palace, and an unoccupied house.

FULFILLMENT

The Grandel Square Theatre is a converted church built in the 1880s. Its east facade is treated with a theatrical flair with light from a row of 250-watt halogen, ground-recessed fixtures that grazes the textured walls. The ghostly aura of the vacant bell tower is created with 250-watt metal halide floodlights fitted with deep blue filters. Theater signage is highlighted by 250-watt halogen PAR spotlights.

Two vacant buildings, the Sun Theatre and Block House, are treated with plays of light. The facade of the Sun Theatre is adorned with 500 feet of neon shaped liked the rays of the sun. The vacant lobbies are lit with spotlights. The east and west facades have a "film noir" effect of shadow and light patterns made with narrow-beam spotlights positioned below the fire escapes. Spotlights backlight the windows of the Block House and one 500-watt spotlight traces a line of oblique light across its facade.

A grass sculpture called "Tilted Planes" that runs toward Grand Avenue from the Grandel Square Theatre is gently highlighted with spill light from nearby historic street lanterns. The diagonal pathway that bisects the sculpture and leads patrons to the parking areas is marked with fiber optics. The illuminators for the fiberoptic cable, which house metal halide lamps, are concealed in vented chambers underneath the grass. Color wheels provide a sequence of four color changes with 20-second fades.

All this exterior lighting is controlled via synchronized time clocks. Long-life halogen lamps also are used for several lighting effects because of their precise control and superior color characteristics.

© 1992 Tony Schanuel

The facade of the Sun Theatre is adorned with 500 feet of neon shaped like the rays of the sun.

Project: **Grandel Square**   Location: **St. Louis, Missouri**   Owner: **Grand Center Inc.**   Architect: **Wedemeyer, Cernik, Carrubia, Inc.**
Lighting Designers: **Randy Burkett and Katherine Abernathy, Randy Burkett Lighting Design, Inc., and Peter Kaczorowski**
Engineer: **Robert Dedeke, Guarantee Electrical Co.**   Graphic Designers: **Kiku Obata, Teresa Bollwerk, Heather Testa, Kiku Obata & Company**
Photographers: © 1992 Tony Schanuel, Courtesy of Randy Burkett Lighting Design, Inc., © Janice K. Broderick
Lighting Manufacturers: **Hydrel**—*burial and accent lights*, **Lumenyte**—*fiber optics*, **Abolite**—*RLMs*, **General Electric Lighting**—*lamps*,
Thorn—*lamps*, and **Tork**—*timeclock controls*

The curbline is illuminated with fiber optics.
The illuminator is hidden beneath the grass.

The facade of the Grandel Square Theatre is
grazed by a row of 250-watt halogen, ground-
mounted fixtures.

GRAND CENTRAL TERMINAL

CRITERIA

The exterior lighting of Grand Central Terminal in Manhattan was part of a $28 million capital improvement plan for the 53-block area around the building, known as the Grand Central Business Improvement District. The 78-year-old terminal building, constructed in the classic Beaux-Arts style, had much to offer in rich sculptural details by night. It was the challenge of Sylvan R. Shemiz Associates to make it a nighttime landmark that would not only do justice to the architecture, but increase the safety and attractiveness of the area for motorists and pedestrians.

FULFILLMENT

The terminal is illuminated with a combination of metal halide and high-pressure sodium (HPS) fixtures mounted on steel racks positioned on roofs and setbacks of four neighboring buildings. The luminaires are mounted on the 16th floor of the Shipcentral Building, the 28th floor of the Bank of America, the 18th floor of the Bowery Savings Bank and the 26th floor of the Lincoln Building.

The throws of light cast from the 136 fixtures are intended to simulate the high position of the sun in mid-summer, when light is unobstructed by the office towers surrounding the terminal.

The 1,000-watt HPS lamps are used for key lighting, to create a sunlight effect with warm, yellow light across the south facade. The blue-hued 1,000-watt metal halide luminaires provide fill light, adding shadows and depth. Arc metal halides add both warm and cool accents on the "Mercury, Hercules, and Minerva" statues and the clock centerpiece, as well as for other sculptural details.

Project: **Grand Central Terminal**   Location: **New York, New York**   Client: **Grand Central Partnership**
Architects: **Jane Thompson, partner-in-charge; James Van Sickle, Diana Tracey, project architects and planners, Benjamin Thompson & Associates**
Lighting Designer: **Sylvan R. Shemitz, principal; Benjamin Stahlheber, senior associate; Joseph Zaharewicz, project manager, Sylvan R. Shemitz Associates**
Photographer: **©1993 Norman McGrath**   Lighting Manufacturers: **GE Lighting, Arc Lighting, Osram Sylvania, Thorn**

The high-pressure sodium lamps create a warm, sunlight effect, and the metal halides offer fill light for a sense of depth and shadow.

ANN ARBOR MAIN STREET

CRITERIA

The tree-lined Main Street of Ann Arbor, Michigan, had been illuminated with rows of 30-35 foot high cobra-head fixtures. "When all those trees are in bloom beneath a 30-foot pole-mounted fixture, no light reaches down underneath the canopy. The merchants were complaining that they didn't have enough business because people were afraid to come downtown at night, and they realized something had to be done," says Gary Steffy, whose firm, Gary Steffy Lighting Design Inc., was called in to redesign the lighting. Johnson, Johnson & Roy/inc was the landscape architect that did it all 25 years ago, so to maintain as much integrity as possible, Johnson, Johnson & Roy/inc, the original landscape architects that had designed Main Street a quarter of a century ago, had been retained to update and freshen the streetscape.

FULFILLMENT

Steffy's firm conducted a series of studies using varied pole heights, and the final decision was made to install 12-foot-high, single-head pole mounted fixtures along the street. "At an intersection, the lighting criteria becomes more critical, with pedestrians crossing and increased traffic. Usually, more light is needed there," says Steffy. Consequently, at intersections, 16-foot-high, multiple-head pole-mounted fixtures are used.

Both versions of the fixtures are lamped with 100-watt, 3200 degree kelvin metal halide sources.

Though some of the detail work is custom, such as the black coloring and mounted details on the head, the fixtures themselves are standard. Steffy notes that the luminaire had been designed by Howard Brandston, H.M Brandston & Partners Inc., for the Park Plaza in downtown Detroit, Michigan, and later adopted into Lumec's standard line. "The optics are good. Most of the light comes down out of the fixture, but some light does go out to the side, so there is a glow cast on tree canopies and building facades."

The lighting designers worked very closely with Johnson, Johnson & Roy/inc. "Johnson, Johnson & Roy/inc. were responsible for all of the construction documentation, as well as for making sure we integrated the lighting layout with whatever street features might be there," Steffy says.

Finally, the lighting team was called on to handle one other minor issue. It was the custom for the local merchants to install lights in the trees for the Christmas season. "But they always seemed to have too few strings and the wrong wattage lamps. Though our major assignment was to create a streetlighting plan that was good for pedestrians and cars all year round, an added part of the assignment was to install tree lights that sort of held their own," comments Steffy. The festive results are clearly visible in the photo!

To maintain the integrity of the streetscape, the original landscape architects were retained to update the area.

Project: **Ann Arbor Main Street**   Location: **Ann Arbor, Michigan**   Landscape Architect: **Johnson, Johnson & Roy/inc**   Lighting Designer: **Gary Steffy Lighting Design Inc.**
Photographer: **© 1993 Robert Eovaldi**   Lighting Manufacturer: **Lumec**

One-hundred-watt metal halide, pole-mounted luminaires adorn the busy avenue, encouraging shoppers to visit local merchants in the evening hours.

MINNESOTA DEPARTMENT OF REVENUE

64

CRITERIA

The Minnesota Department of Revenue building anchors the south side development of the Mississippi River area in downtown St. Paul. Lighting designer Patty Yorks had the challenge of creating a dramatic design that would unify the parking lot, ring-road drive, exterior courtyard, building facade, and interior atrium, and establish a positive public image for the building.

Considerations included maintaining smooth transitions from one area to another in light levels and visual impact of the selected fixtures, and in meeting city lighting standards, along with public expectation for efficient and tasteful lighting of a government building.

The lack of building-mounted luminaires preserves the clean, straight lines of the facade.

FULFILLMENT

The city's streetlighting standard is a traditional style, turn-of-the-century globe-type luminaire, augmented with the power company's cobra-head floodlights. In the courtyard and roadway areas, an average of 0.5 foot-candles, required by the city, has been accomplished with a uniformity ratio of 3:1 by using three-globe fixtures fitted with 50-watt high-pressure sodium (HPS) lamps, without any augmentation. Five-globe fixtures have been installed to distinguish points of entry.

These traditional-style pole-mounted luminaires have intentionally been situated away from the building to allow for a more clean-lined treatment for the sleek, architecturally modern structure.

The central spine of the building is stepped, from one to three to nine stories. The designer has used HPS sources in combinations of 250-, 400-, and 1,000-watts and fitted with pink filters to cast warm, complementary light upon the carnelian granite inset in the building's facade.

The HPS fixtures are mounted in low-profile, freestanding granite boxes situated on the ground to light the facade, and mounted unobtrusively on low planter walls to cast light down onto the walkways. The lack of building-mounted luminaires preserves the smooth, straight lines of the structure. The fixtures achieve an average of 10 footcandles, with a uniformity ratio of 2:1 in the one-to-three story area.

This project is particularly interesting because it has combined pleasing aesthetics with excellent energy efficiency. By using energy-efficient fixtures, lamps and ballasts, the owner qualified for a rebate from Northern States Power totalling nearly $15,000 for the entire project. Annual operating costs for the street lighting are $40 per fixture; for the exterior courtyard, $20 per fixture, and for the exterior facade lighting, $1,000 total.

The facade is lit with ground-mounted, energy-efficient high-pressure sodium fixtures.

Project: **Minnesota Department of Revenue**   Location: **St. Paul, Minnesota**   Client: **Minnesota Department of Revenue**
Lighting Designer: **Patricia Yorks, ASID, IALD, Lighting By Patricia Yorks Designs, Inc.**
Photographer: **Terry Anderson, Silker Anderson Photography** Photos are provided courtesy of Sterner Lighting
Lighting Manufacturers: **Sterner Lighting, Bega, Kim Lighting, Kurt Versen, Osram Sylvania**

The stepped central spine is lit with high-pressure sodium lamps fitted with pink filters to complement the carnelian granite inset.

The pole-mounted roadway luminaires are situated away from the building to preserve the structure's streamlined aesthetics.

CHAPTER 2

PARKS AND PLAZAS

The lighting for parks and plazas has to mix beauty with real-world considerations: vandal-proofing, safety, glare control, avoidance of light trespass, and the production of a public area that complements, and does not overwhelm, the surrounding environment.

This chapter contains projects which present varied approaches to welcoming the public. Pole-mounted fixtures that also function as decorative banner-holders illuminate Riverwalk, the rehabilitated downtown riverfront area in Fort Lauderdale, Florida.

Yokohama's Grand Mall Park is a hub for artistic activities held day and night during all seasons. Visitors to the park at night can experience the excitement of walking on thousands of twinkling lights embedded in the ground. A similar experience can be had by pedestrians walking across the plaza at Renaissance Square in Phoenix, Arizona, where a 16-point star of light is embedded in the ground surrounding an illuminated clock tower.

Mill Race Park relies on burial units and unobtrusive recessed fixtures to highlight the water feature, plantings and stone wall-mounted artworks. And at Jefferson Park Gazebo, pole-mounted pathway gaslight-style luminaires are combined with vandal-resistant fluorescent fixtures that light the gazebo itself for night performances.

JEFFERSON PARK GAZEBO

CRITERIA

Jefferson Park, located in a designated historic district of Columbus, Ohio, includes the former home of early-twentieth-century American writer James Thurber. In front of the house, in the north side of the park, is a bronze statue of a unicorn inspired by one of Thurber's most popular stories, "The Unicorn in the Garden."

Steven Elbert, AIA, entered a competition sponsored by the American Institute of Architects (AIA) to design a gazebo for the park that would extend its historic character. It also had to be vandal-resistant, sturdy, and virtually maintenance-free to fend off harsh environmental conditions.

Elbert met the requirements for the park's structure with a touch of whimsy, adding a multi-faceted lighting system that extends the ability to use the gazebo into the nighttime hours. The gazebo project was awarded to him as a result of his winning first place in the AIA-sponsored competition.

FULFILLMENT

Steven Elbert's concept situates the gazebo at the south end of the park in the midst of a grassy knoll, as a visual counterpoint to the unicorn statue.

"Locating the gazebo on the edge of the park also maximizes the seating area and side-steps high tension lines running through the center of the park," says Elbert. "The conductor's podium has a western exposure, so those attending a concert are facing east during sunset performances." The gazebo is visible from the principle east-west street of the city as well.

The 26-foot diameter gazebo is visually tied to the unicorn statue via a spiraling motif. The double helix spire at the top of the gazebo mimics the gentle twisting of the unicorn's horn. The spire, fabricated by local sculptor David Bamber, is made of structural steel rods twisted and welded together.

Durable, industrial-type materials chosen to withstand frequent use and deter vandalism are used throughout the construction of the gazebo. "The theme of the twisting spire is continued in the columns, which are sewer pipes filled with concrete, so if vandals draw on them with a marker, the columns can be wiped clean with a paper towel," says Elbert. Other structural elements are made of steel and slate. The clear window panels are made of Lexan.

Most of the light fixtures have been unobtrusively integrated into the structure. The general lighting in the gazebo comes from two sources. Set around the perimeter of the octagonal roof are 16 cool-white fluorescents concealed behind vandal-resistant, gridded steel screen housings painted white. The second source is an industrial-style, 400-watt metal halide fixture suspended at the gazebo's center and protected by a vandal-resistant Lexan lens.

The lozenge-shaped fixture above the conductor's podium has been rendered vandal proof and weather resistant by a protective steel cage and waterproof O-ring seal. The standard incandescent lamp in the fixture has been substituted with a compact fluorescent 26-watt lamp to conserve energy and minimize relamping.

The spire is lit by a waterproof-lensed, mercury vapor unit set just beneath it that casts illumination straight up. The fixture is on a timer that turns it on at sunset and off about 2:00 A.M.

All lights can be turned on for use from an electrical panel box near the gazebo. If additional lighting is needed, equipment can be accommodated by the numerous outlets in the floor and ceiling, which have weatherproof housings and are under keylock to prevent electrical accidents.

The surrounding grassy areas and walkways are illuminated at night by 18 pole-mounted gaslight fixtures. Columbia Gas Company of Ohio has donated the Welsbach gaslight fixtures, along with their cleaning and maintenance.

The construction cost for the gazebo was $129,000, a reasonable sum considering the many functions served by the structure. The gazebo has helped revitalize the area by promoting public use of the park. It is used as an entertainment area where poetry readings, music, dance and dramatic performances are scheduled. Students at an adjacent college use the area for lunching and outdoor classes, while local residents enjoy it as a lovely setting for wedding and prom photo sessions.

Upon the completion of the gazebo, Steven Elbert was granted an AIA Honor Award.

Project: **Jefferson Park Gazebo**   Location: **Columbus, Ohio**
Owner: **City of Columbus, Ohio**   Architect: **Steven M. Elbert, AIA**
Lighting Designers: **Steven M. Elbert, AIA, and Leonard Kolada, AIA**
Contractor: **Whetstone Construction Co.**
Photographer: **© Lumen Architectural Photography**
Lighting Manufacturers: **Lithonia**—*metal halide fixture & fluorescent strips,* **Prisma Illuminazione Co.**—*lozenge-shaped fixture,* **Hadco**—*mercury vapor spire fixture,* **Columbia Gas Co. of Ohio**—*donated natural gas lighting fixtures,* **Welsbach**—*manufacturer of natural gas lighting fixtures*

The 18 pole-mounted gaslight fixtures have been donated, along with their cleaning and maintenance, by Columbia Gas Company of Ohio.

The fluorescent fixtures have been painted white and gently wash the white-painted underside of the roof.

The fixture above the conductor's podium has been fitted with a long-life compact fluorescent lamp.

The historical character of the park is enhanced at night by the gaslight pole-mounted fixtures that illuminate the walkways surrounding the gazebo.

Attached to the perimeter of the underside of the octagonal roof are fluorescent fixtures with steel screen, vandal-proof housings.

A mercury vapor fixture uplights the spire. Beneath it, a metal halide fixture set in the center of the roof provides illumination in the gazebo.

The gazebo's double helix spire mimics the spiraling horn of the park's bronze unicorn statue.

RENAISSANCE SQUARE

CRITERIA

Renaissance Square is a full city block, mixed use development of over one million square feet. Its name reflects the hopes of city inhabitants and officials to revitalize downtown Phoenix. The northeast quarter of the square includes a new civic plaza, situated between Patriot's Park and what is planned to be a future pedestrian mall.

Phoenix is a city of sunshine, and one of the goals of lighting designer, Craig A. Roeder, IES, IALD, was to help visitors adjust from walking in the intense bright daylight into the building interiors by day. To ease this transition, light levels had to step down from plaza to the building cores.

At night, the lighting had to project a feeling of safety and comfort, clearly indicate circulation areas in indoor and outdoor spaces, and draw pedestrian traffic to retail areas.

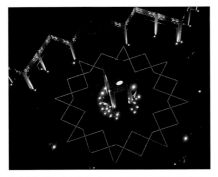

Set into the joints between the granite paving blocks in the plaza are mini-lamp strips that form a 16-point star pattern.

FULFILLMENT

The focal point of the plaza is a clock tower surrounded by a 16-point star created with polycarbonate mini-lamp channel strips embedded in the joints between the granite paving blocks. The light star, animated by chase controllers, is particularly enjoyed by occupants of the two adjacent high-rise office buildings, who can view the show from their office windows.

Why a 16-point star? "Eight is one of the two divine numbers," explains Craig Roeder. Combining two eight-point stars creates a cosmic symbol that represents material power and wealth.

Several buildings were demolished—including one with Art Deco detailing—so that Renaissance Square could be built. Fortunately, the developer preserved decorative precast concrete panels from the building's facade. These original panels and additional replications have been mounted on the facade of a retail pavilion at the corner of the plaza.

Roeder has opted to backlight the panels, which are detailed with cast openings, with 3000 degree Kelvin fluorescent strips concealed behind frosted acrylic panels to produce a diffuse light. To balance this band of light, custom burial uplights have been recessed around the pavilion's outer columns.

The burial units contain 250-watt, halogen PAR 38 lamps and are fitted with 3-inch-deep internal black matte louvers to reduce glare. Adjustable recessed fixtures also using 250-watt PAR 38s are aimed down along columns from the two-story ceilings of the entrances to the high rises.

Glass color filters can be added to all the PAR fixtures to create festive seasonal and holiday atmospheres.

The developer requested a dramatic soffit with exposed structure in the entrance lobby, so the architect, Emery Roth, designed ribbed groin vaults, modified after consulting with Roeder, to incorporate double ribs, so lighting fixtures could be concealed between them. This allowed inexpensive two-circuit track equipment to be used.

All the ground-level public space circulation lighting—tree uplights, tree-mounted downlights shielded with louvers and hoods, landscape and fountain fixtures, plaza and building lobby lighting—is automatically controlled by an astronomical time-based energy management system. Two eight-scene preset dimming systems respond to the clock by changing light levels as the day goes on. All incandescent lighting is dimmed by at least 20 percent to increase lamp life.

The revitalizing theme of Renaissance Square is embodied in the high-rise entrance sculpture called "Full Life Reach" and created by Trevor Southey. To promote an added sense of drama around the artwork, sandblasted stripes were added in the polished granite column cladding to catch and reflect light.

Project: **One and Two Renaissance Square**   Location: **Phoenix, Arizona**
Developer: **Trammell Crow Co.**   Lighting Designer: **Craig A. Roeder Associates, Inc.**
Architect: **Emery Roth & Sons**   Associate Architects: **Harwood K. Smith & Partners;**
Pierce, Goodwin & Alexander; James, Harwich + Partners
Photographers: **Robert Ames Cook, Greg Hursley**
Lighting Manufacturers: **Hydrel, Litelab, Edison Price Lighting, Norbert Belfer Lighting**

Color filters added to the PAR uplights add a
festive touch to the area surrounding the
"Full Life Reach" sculpture.

All incandescent lighting is dimmed at least 20
percent to extend lamp life. The uplights are
custom-made and flush with the ground.

Precast decorative panels, salvaged from an Art
Deco building that had to be demolished to
make way for Renaissance Square, are backlit
with fluorescent strips to emphasize their ornate
detailing.

GRAND MALL PARK

CRITERIA

The Grand Mall Park is located in the center of Yokohama's redevelopment project, called "Minato Mirai 21," between Sakuragicho station and Yokohama Bay. With the adjacent Yokohama Museum of Art, the park is expected to become a central hub for artistic activities to be held, day and night, and in all seasons. It was used as part of the fairgrounds for the Yokohama Exotic Showcase, a special event held for six months beginning in March 1989.

An innovative nighttime image to be created with light was needed for the park in keeping with the flourishing art events to be held there.

FULFILLMENT

By adopting innovative lighting methods, an image of a future-city park was created. The lighting concept evolved around expressing the harmony among light, water and greenery, as well as revealing the city of Yokohama's individuality.

In the central plaza, 1,040 pieces of Yakohkai Pave (900 millimeters square) were laid out in an area 20 meters long and 100 meters wide. These were developed by combining solar modules and LEDs to represent the image of the sea glowing in the dark. No fixtures are visible in order to take advantage of the Yakohkai Pave. Indirect lighting was used for uplighting adjacent trees, walls, benches, and water features.

To promote outdoor activities, two automatic height-controllable poles on which stage lights have been mounted are installed in the ground.

In the central plaza, 1,040 pieces of Yakohkai Pave were laid out. These were developed by combining solar modules and LEDs to create an image of the sea glowing in the dark.

Project: **Yokohama Minato Mirai 21, Grand Mall Park**   Location: **Yokohama, Tokyo**   Lighting Designer: **Motoko Ishii, Motoko Ishii Lighting Design Inc.**
Photographer: **Yoichi Yamazaki**

Structures, trees and benches are uplit so as not to distract from the LED-lit plaza they surround.

RIVERWALK

CRITERIA

Many years ago, strings of bare bulbs had laced the riverbanks of the New River in Fort Lauderdale, Florida. But in recent years, the banks had been underutilized and so to revitalize the area, the City of Fort Lauderdale commissioned Edward D. Stone, Jr. & Associates to plan a multi-phase project that would attract pedestrian activity and subsequently promote economic development downtown.

Known as Riverwalk, this reborn area is designed to unify the diverse sections along the riverfront, while allowing each to maintain its own unique character. Furnishings and materials have been selected to carry through traditional, yet undated themes, that also embody some flexible options in application.

The lighting system was an important and integral part of this project's development, since through nighttime illumination messages of safety, security, comfort and the presence of a relaxing, enjoyable atmosphere could be conveyed.

FULFILLMENT

One phase of the project involved the creation of a one-mile linear park that winds along the New River. Bob Dugan, project manager, says, "We chose the lights as the unifying element to give the linear park a sense of place. The lights themselves become beacons. If you follow the path of the lights, you will find Riverwalk. They are very distinct and have become the identifying feature of the entire area."

To maintain a sense of tradition, yet establish a look that would remain undated as time passed, a classic, turn-of-the-century fiberglass lamp post design was selected and adapted for the project. The lamp posts, spaced anywhere from 40-70 feet apart, are only about 11 feet high, relatively small in scale, so that sufficient illumination can be provided beneath the heavy shade canopies of the many existing and relocated trees. The low mounting height and repetition of the fixtures also creates the pleasing "necklace of light" visual image when viewed from a distance.

The textured, spatter finish on the posts resembles cast iron, yet limits reflection and is weatherproof, requiring little maintenance in the highly humid climate. The deep blue-green color of the lamp posts and shades, called by those involved in the project "Riverwalk blue," is carried through on other park-related materials and furnishings, such as benches, sunshades, graphics and maintenance uniforms.

"The direct burial approach saves us money on footings so we were able to put more back into our budget for the fixtures themselves," says Dugan. The luminaires contain 100-watt, frosted metal halide lamps enclosed in milk-white glass globes that protect the light sources and prevent glare.

The area contains a variety of facilities—including a performing arts center, and office buildings in a two-block historic district—and the lighting fixtures serve visually to unify and connect the diverse architecture. The style of the standards is also varied—some posts contain light fixtures only, some hold decorative banners, and others carry a combination of lights and banners. However, electrical receptacles are included in all the posts for festival and holiday use.

When the five phases of this 28-acre park project are complete, approximately 150 to 200 pole-mounted luminaires will have been installed.

Edward D. Stone, Jr. & Associates has been granted the 1992 Frederic B. Stresau Award for Excellence by the Florida Chapter of the American Society of Landscape Architects (ASLA) in recognition of the concept and design of this project.

Project: **Riverwalk**   Location: **Fort Lauderdale, Florida**
Client: **City of Fort Lauderdale, Florida**
Landscape Architect & Lighting Designer: **Edward D. Stone, Jr. & Associates,**
Robert Dugan, project manager
Photographer: **Courtesy of Edward D. Stone, Jr. & Associates**
Lighting Manufacturers: **Street Lighting Equipment Corporation, W.J. Whatley, Inc.**

The spatter finish on the fiberglass poles has been dubbed "Riverwalk blue."

Frosted metal halide lamps are enclosed in milk-white globes to protect the light source and prevent glare.

The repetition of fixtures creates a "necklace of light" along the banks of the New River.

The fiberglass poles and textured finish are resistant to damage from the humid climate.

MILL RACE PARK

CRITERIA

Before concrete structures rose to form the downtown of Battle Creek, Michigan, there had existed a Mill Race, constructed in the mid-nineteenth century by Sans McCamly between two rivers to provide a waterway for milling operations, and so promote industry. The Kellogg Foundation, which planned to construct an office building near the former site of the Mill Race, decided to give something back to the city of Battle Creek, and so created a pocket park—Mill Race Park—across the street from the office building, that recognizes and preserves this aspect of important local history.

FULFILLMENT

The main feature of the park is a water wall and run, reminiscent of the original Mill Race.

"The water pours over the top of the wall, and then down through the run, which is about the same width as the original Mill Race," says George Sass, principal in charge of design and engineering, Johnson, Johnson & Roy/inc. "The side walls are built of fieldstone, as were the walls of the race. The bed of the original Mill Race would have been dirt, but without using a great depth of water, we wanted to create some ripple action in the water itself, so we installed a surface that would do that." A bed of dark gray stones are set at an angle to make the water ripple as it flows over them.

The water used in the run is recycled continuously. When the pumps are turned off in the winter, the water is stored in a holding tank below ground.

The vertical stone wall behind the water stretches out, water-free, to the left and right of the run, and serves as the backdrop for a series of three-dimensional sculptures by Timothy Woodman. The artworks depict the story, from left to right, of the Mill Race from the clearing of the woodland, to the opening of the water channel. The wall also creates a sense of privacy and quiet, shielding the park strollers form the surrounding bustling, business environment. On either side of the water run are open walkways and planting beds.

The decision to opt for recessed rather than pole-mounted lighting fixtures was an intentional one. "That was something that we and the landscape architects felt very strongly about," says Gary Woodall, project designer at Gary Steffy Lighting Design Inc. "We wanted the main feature of the park to be the water wall. Any sort of vertical element in the park would detract from the wall and be distracting."

Though all the lighting is recessed, the units and light sources used vary. Burial units fitted with 250-watt, PAR 38 quartz incandescent reflector lamps, are placed single file in front of the walls to highlight the artworks. On the bridge over the water run, integrated into the handrailing detail, are 90-watt incandescent A-lamp uplights with etched glass lenses that provide a soft glow and highlight the pathway across the bridge.

To illuminate the water wall, underwater-rated quartz 250-watt, PAR 38 fixtures are installed in the stone bed beneath the water run. The rippling water is made to shimmer with 50-watt, PAR 20 units in 4-inch diameter housings recessed in the side stone walls.

The plantings are lighted with the same 4-inch diameter lights, but instead of a lens, a case louver is fitted onto the fixtures in the path areas. And, instead of incandescent sources, the tree uplights use deluxe white mercury vapor lamps.

Easy access is gained to all units by unscrewing the lenses and louvers from the top for relamping. To allay concerns about water leakage, the design team visited the manufacturer for demonstrations. The fixtures used, according to Woodall, combine underwater pool lighting technology with in-ground, uplight housings.

There were sound reasons why the lighting team chose incandescent sources for this project, rather than high-intensity discharge sources typically used in outdoor lighting. "For time-of-day dimming control, for candlepower versus wattage and luminaire size, and for maintenance, the incandescent sources made a lot of sense for this particular project. Also, the park is a public amenity provided by the Kellogg Foundation, and as such it should embody a universal appeal—something incandescent does quite well," says Gary Steffy, IALD, principal, Gary Steffy Lighting Design Inc.

The dimming system allows the wall to change appearance during the evening via changes in light levels. Groups of lights are placed on independent channels, so, for example, the left and right sides of the wall, and the water wall under the bridge can each be controlled separately.

"Regarding energy efficiency, the nearest equivalent light source we could have used to produce the same intensity of light on the wall would have been the 175-watt metal halide lamp. Given the fact that we have dimmed back the incandescent units, our input watts would be about the same for metal halide as they are for the incandescent," says Woodall.

"We also wanted to tell a color story. The mercury vapor fixtures have been chosen to highlight the trees because they enhance the blue-green quality of the plantings," says Woodall. "The incandescent lighting cast on the wall allows the stone to take on a warm, inviting appearance."

Mill Race park was opened to the public in October 1991.

Project: **Mill Race Park**   Location: **Battle Creek, Michigan**
Owners: **W.K. Kellog Foundation, and the city of Battle Creek**
Lighting Designer: **Gary Steffy Lighting Design Inc.**
Photographer: **© 1993 Robert Eovaldi**   Landscape Architect: **Johnson, Johnson & Roy/inc**   Electrical Engineer: **Neil Adams, Inc.**
General Contractor: **Granger Corporation**   Lighting Manufacturers: **Hydrel—*in-pavement and tree up-lights;* Sterner Lighting Systems, Inc.—*step lighting***

Since the water run is the main feature of
the park, distracting vertically-mounted fixtures
have been avoided. The water in the run is
recycled continuously.

In the bridge's handrailing, 90-watt incandescent A-lamp uplights with etched glass lenses have been integrated to highlight the pathway.

A shimmering effect is created by the illumination from uplights and sidelights interplaying with the moving water.

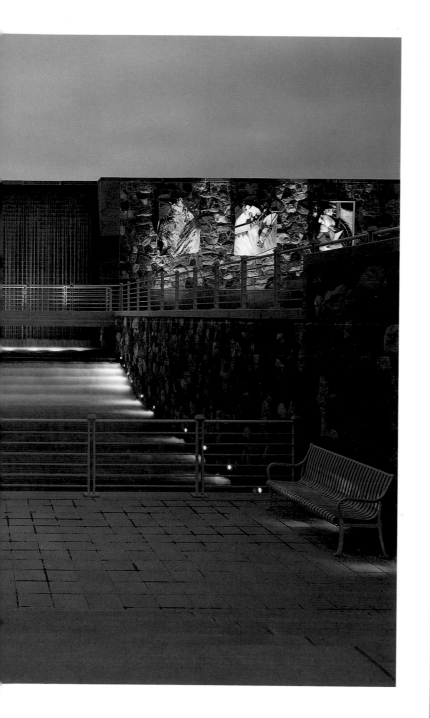

Though several options had been considered, incandescent fixtures—in-ground, 250-watt, PAR 38 units—have been chosen to make the artwork-adorned stone wall appear warm and inviting.

CHAPTER 3

CORPORATE
BUILDINGS

Projecting an appropriate corporate image by means of exterior lighting for a headquarters building can be accomplished in many ways, as demonstrated in this chapter. The "image" often translates into lighting viewed long distance as part of the cityscape. Striking acrylic-shielded green neon, for example, encircles the hexagons at the top of the Emerald-Shapery Center and Pan Pacific Hotel. Selective highlighting of the architectural features distinguishes Fleet National Bank and BP America from their skyscraper neighbors in the nighttime urban landscape.

Oftentimes, limitations in where fixtures can be located influence the exterior lighting. This is the case in the selection of powerful xenon searchlights that adorn the streamlined facade of the NEC headquarters in Tokyo with sweeping shafts of light.

Animated lighting is a concept used more frequently today in establishing attention-getting corporate images. Chasing lights promote the rocketship-like appearance of Interstate Tower, and beams from custom pylons move beams across the landscape sculpture at Regent Court to mimic the sun's movement.

Often, the lighting professional must connect the exterior building lighting with pedestrian-accessed plazas and entryways. Strong visual connections between the building architecture and the ground-level public areas are made at Landmark Centre and Prudential Plaza via the lighting.

The bioMerieux Vitek structure builds its image from within, as well as from without, creating a nighttime look by combining interior-lit stairwells visible through window walls, and vertical shafts of light emanating from exterior-mounted fixtures. Lighting can mean ornate decoration as well, and this is the case at New England Telephone, where exterior facade treatments and sconces have been created to complement the Art Deco style of the architecture.

EMERALD-SHAPERY CENTER
AND PAN PACIFIC HOTEL

CRITERIA

The Emerald-Shapery Center and Pan Pacific Hotel in downtown San Diego are part of a 700,000 square foot, mixed use development at 402 West Broadway in San Diego. The Emerald-Shapery Center is comprised of eight hexagonal modules that rise to varying heights designed to represent an organic crystalline form. The five northern modules comprise a steel office-building structure that includes a 30-story tower. The three southern modules that front Broadway form the 436-unit concrete hotel structure with a 27-story tower.

The office and hotel complexes are connected by a 100-foot high glass atrium with roof structures at the sixth and eighth floors. Bridge balconies tie the second and third floor hotel function areas together, allowing access to the meeting rooms and ballrooms that open onto the atrium.

The complex's architect, C.W. Kim, AIA, drew on American architect, Frank Lloyd Wright's philosophy of imitating natural formations in architecture to create the organic shapes and angled, glass tower tops that mimic an emerald crystal growing from a solid mineral base.

Lighting developed for the complex had to build on the architectural concept, and be easy to maintain and energy efficient as well.

Project: **Emerald-Shapery Center**   Location: **San Diego, California**
Client/Owner: **Shapery Enterprises and San Diego 109, Inc.,**
a subsidiary of Tokyu Corporation of Japan
Lighting Designer: **John H. Anderson & Associates**
Lighting Conceptual Consultation: **William Lam Associates, Inc.**   Architect: **C.W. Kim, AIA**
Photographer: **Stephen Whalen, Stephen Whalen Photography, Del Mar, California**
Lighting Manufacturers: **Rohm and Haas Company**—*Plexiglas DR acrylic (Plexiglas and DR are registered trademarks)*; **Sandee Advanced Thermoplastic Extrusions**—*design and manufacture of Plexiglas shields*; **Signtech Electical Advertising, Inc.**—*manufacture and installation of neon tubing and of Plexiglas shields*

FULFILLMENT

William Lam provided conceptual consultation on the lighting in the project's preliminary stage, with John H. Anderson serving as the project lighting consultant.

The lighting elements which encircle the hexagonal tower tops include green neon combined with cylindrical covers made of transparent acrylic shielding. The combination creates diffuse bands of light that form luminous hexagons, rather than the stark outlines which would have been produced by using exposed neon alone.

The green of the neon enhanced the image of the Emerald-Shapery Center, and provided a refreshing contrast to the existing blue and red signage in the city's skyline. Neon was selected because the transformers are less obtrusive than those used for low-voltage light tubes, and the expected lamp life of neon tubing is a minimum of 10 years. In addition, all outdoor luminous tube lighting fixtures are exempt from the requirement of the Palomar Observatory lighting code, which limits the brightness of outdoor lighting within 100 miles of Mount Palomar (San Diego is approximately 90 miles away)—at the time of construction.

To create the illusion of larger bands of light, the 2,000 feet of $5/8$ inch diameter neon tubing was covered with 3-inch diameter extruded transparent Plexiglas shield refractors. The U-shaped configuration of the acrylic shielding emits lumens into a directed source at the parapet cap, reflecting and enlarging the image of the neon tubes. The neon tubes emit more than 440,000 lumens, according to Anderson.

By using the extruded Plexiglas for the shielding, the designer was able to use one-half of the originally planned lumens per foot of tube for lighting the parapets. "We originally planned to use 60 mA current," says Anderson, "but the ability to easily shape the lens to an optimum configuration for lumen refraction dispersal permitted a reduction to 30 mA." Total wattage for exterior neon lighting is approximately 7 kilowatts, or 146 watts per 40-foot tube section x 6 sides x 8 modules.

The shielding is durable and offers up to 10 times the impact resistance of standard acrylics. It stands up to a range of weather conditions without the need for special ultraviolet coatings.

Acrylic shielding also helps insure safety. According to the San Diego City Building Department, the National Electrical Code requires that all outline lighting constructed with exposed neon must be installed no less than 8 feet above a finished grade. The shields protect neon tubes from damage by natural elements, and prevent contact of high-voltage tubes with maintenance workers and window washers, and with office workers and hotel guests on balconies.

This southeast view shows the three hotel modules with the 27-story tower in the foreground, and the five office modules with the 30-story tower in the background.

The plexiglass encasement for the green neon strips provides protection from environmental and safety hazards.

A close-up appreciation of the neon lighting can be achieved from a high point in the Emerald-Shapery complex.

Green neon provides a striking contrast with the existing blue and red signs in the city's skyline.

The hexagonal design is based on Frank Lloyd Wright's philosophy of imitating natural formations in architecture.

The shield refractors create the illusion from a distance that the neon banding is thicker than it really is.

BP AMERICA

CRITERIA

Though the building is currently owned by the British Petroleum America group (BP America), it originally was built, and the exterior illumination commissioned, by Standard Oil of Ohio (SOHIO).

SOHIO representatives requested the building not attract attention with over-bright illumination, but rather present a quality image for the company through subtle and elegant lighting. The lighting design accomplished for SOHIO has been maintained by BP America.

The client requested subtle, elegant illumination for the granite-clad structure.

FULFILLMENT

The project was complex for several reasons. Because the granite facade was not rendered satisfactorily with either metal halide or high-pressure (HPS) sources, a mixture of both was decided upon, requiring the installation of a duplicate set of fixtures to accommodate the two sources.

The fixtures that illuminate the vertical setbacks are mounted on the flat rooftops of the atrium. The custom-designed fixtures have a complex reflector design that helps achieve the long illumination throws of over 300 feet. "A couple of the fixtures were literally the size of bathtubs," says Randy Burkett, with Hellmuth, Obata & Kassabaum, Inc. at the time of the project, and now president of Randy Burkett Lighting Design. "It was also important to restrict light from hitting the center of the building. The concept was to light the side stepbacks, but not allow much spill light in the center of the building facade, because there was a concern that if it was evenly illuminated, it would look flat—like a tombstone. So using louvers, we occluded as much of the light as possible from the central bay."

The horizontal stepbacks that cap the building are lit with three different light sources to differentiate it from what is below. The third added source is mercury housed in fixtures fitted with green louvers.

Because of the complexity of the mixing of multiple light sources, the louvering and the long throws, this project took about one week to aim.

Since these photos were taken, the back of the building has been illuminated as well. At the time of the front facade illumination, there was no place to mount the fixtures because the clients, at the time, didn't own the property behind the building.

Project: **BP America (formerly SOHIO)**   Client: **Standard Oil of Ohio**   Location: **Cleveland, Ohio**   Architect: **James J. McDonald, Hellmuth, Obata & Kassabaum, Inc.**
Lighting Designer: **Randy Burkett, at the time of the project with Hellmuth, Obata & Kassabaum Inc., and currently president of Randy Burkett Lighting Design, Inc.**
Photographer: **Courtesy of HOK Photography**   Lighting Manufacturer: **Sterner Lighting**

Stepbacks are highlighted with a mix of metal
halide and high-pressure sodium fixtures.
Mercury has been added to the light source
combination at the top of the building.

LANDMARK CENTRE

CRITERIA

Landmark Centre, which is situated on a 200-foot by 200-foot city block, is the first building in Tampa to have another office tower next to it on an adjacent block.

"The structure is a contemporary expression of classical building elements: a base, containing the ground floor lobby and parking levels; a middle, containing the office floors; and a top, developed with two penthouse office floors and the ziggurat roof," says Steven M. Berberich, AIA, Cooper Carry & Associates, Inc., the architects on the project. "As a good citizen to the city, the base as experienced at the pedestrian level, and the top as viewed from a distance, are oriented to respect and reinforce the urban planning street grid. Office floors are rotated 45 degrees to provide vistas from within of Tampa Bay and the downtown past the adjacent high-rise building."

The collaborative efforts of Cooper Carry & Associates, Inc., lighting designers Fisher Marantz Renfro Stone, and custom manufacturer Cornelius Architectural Products have developed a lighting scheme that reinforces the impact of the building's architecture.

FULFILLMENT

The ziggurat roof structure is illuminated with fluorescents positioned all around the base of each of the steps. The building owner has the option of fitting the fluorescent tubes with filters to mark holidays and special occasions.

The circles of light that line the perimeter of the top of each rotated section of the building are "jelly jars" with aluminum caps that prevent direct view of the filament.

"In an urban context a building has two primary views: the pedestrian view, and the distant view as part of the skyline," says Richard Renfro, Fisher Marantz Renfro Stone Lighting Design. The lighting elements viewed by pedestrians at the front entrance are totally integrated with the distant, skyline image of the building. A procession of eight torchieres (four on each side) flank the path leading to the entance between two sunken, landscaped public park areas.

"The torchieres are a good example of how light and architecture can work together," says Renfro. The aluminum torchieres are distinguished by pyramidal acrylic and aluminum tops which mimic the building's roof structure. The torchieres are uplit by metal halide garden fixtures concealed in the square, 2½-foot-high granite bases. The uplight not only allows the top of the torchiere to appear self-illuminating, but it casts a glow of spill light onto pathway and park areas.

Renfro says, "The imagery of the pathway between the garden areas as a bridge leading to the building struck me, and led to the concept of the torchieres as a procession of markers across the bridge that bring you to the front door."

"There were special requirements to be considered in creating the torchieres," explains Mark Rothert, Cornelius Architectural Products. "We had the choice of either cutting the vertical legs from solid plate or fabricating them from tube. We chose to fabricate the parts from 1 1/2 by 2 inch rectangular tubing.

"The three vertical pieces in each leg of the fixture are tied together with square metal sections that depict a large square formed by a pattern of four smaller ones. We couldn't have any plastic adhesives or body-filler showing where the pieces had been joined. Everything had to be welded and ground flush because people could walk right up to these and touch them," says Rothert.

The four vertical legs culminate in a pyramid at the top underscored by three levels of acrylic that appear to be panels intersecting the vertical legs. Actually the 1-inch thick, sandblasted acrylic has been cut into four L-shaped pieces that have been set into an aluminum frame to hold them in place.

Cornelius Architectural Products was already involved in the project manufacturing ornate railings, signage, building directories and other elements. Renfro points out, "Usually, if a project requires specialized custom fixture work, this can limit the field of who can do the work quickly. The torchieres didn't require special internal wiring. The idea here is that the custom lighting fixtures can be part of the architectural metal package, and that can make for more competitive bidding."

At the same time, the city of Tampa had put into effect an ordinance that requires a percentage of the building to be dedicated to art. "Although the Landmark Centre project was begun before that ordinance took effect, we felt we wanted to contribute to the spirit of it and these torchieres do that, because they are artful sculptural elements," says Berberich.

Project: **Landmark Centre**   Location: Tampa, Florida
Client: **The Landmarks Group, Atlanta, GA: Bart Abstein**, senior vice president of development, and **Gary Minor**, project manager
Architect: **Kevin Cantley**, design director, and **Steven M. Berberich**, project architect, Cooper Carry & Associates, Inc.
Lighting Designer: **Richard Renfro**, design principal, and **Melanie Freundlich**, project manager, Fisher Marantz Renfro Stone Lighting Design
Photographer: © 1993 E. Alan McGee, Atlanta   Lighting Manufacturer: **Cornelius Architectural Products, Mark Rothert**, project manager

"Jelly jar" fixtures with aluminum caps line the perimeter of each rotated section of the structure.

Fluorescent fixtures are positioned at the base of the steps that surround the ziggurat roof.

The aluminum and acrylic torchieres are uplit by metal halide garden fixtures concealed in the granite bases.

PRUDENTIAL PLAZA

CRITERIA

The challenge for the architecture and design team at Loebl Schlossman and Hackl, Inc., was to renovate the existing 41-story Prudential tower, and design a new 64-story tower with a new adjacent, one-acre public plaza to make Chicago's Prudential Plaza a first-class office complex.

A common mezzanine and two 5-story atriums join the old rectangular building, built in 1953, with the new building completed in 1989. The materials and design patterns in the interiors of the lobby and mezzanine also match.

The specific concept for the lighting design was based on the unusual architecture of the new Two Prudential Plaza building. The top of the building is graduated, with 15-foot setbacks. "The multi-planed structure made it a natural idea to install illumination where the setbacks occur to create accentuations with light and shadow. There was no attempt to wash entire walls, only those portions where the contrast would be most pronounced so the building's form could be clearly seen," says Johnson.

The cladding of the new Two Prudential Plaza, the fifth tallest building in Chicago and the tallest reinforced concrete building in the world, complements the existing building's limestone and aluminum skin.

FULFILLMENT

The lighting adorns primarily the north and south facades of the new building. The east and west facades aren't illuminated because they are flat surfaces.

At the top of the building, the horizontal lines of light are created by 175-watt metal halide lamps that cast light up onto white-painted aluminum panel reflectors. The reflectors create a uniform banding and shield light from spilling onto the adjacent panels of reflective glass.

Before the spire was illuminated, it had already been painted silver and could not be repainted. So on each of the four sides of the tall, thin, pyramidal spire is a 1,000-watt metal halide fixture uplighting it.

The graduated setbacks are also highlighted with 175-watt metal halides. "The fixtures are directed virtually straight up in order to create a long, thin line of light to accentuate and show off the granite.

The fixtures are set away from the building slightly, with a shallow angle of incidence—perhaps 2 to 5 degrees set off from a plumb

vertical line toward the building," says Johnson. Operable windows on each of the roofs open for repair and maintenance of the equipment.

The plaza lighting, including lanterns incorporated into the building columns, was a significant part of the project from the beginning. "The plaza, on the north side of the building, is usually in shade," says Johnson. "And in Chicago there are a lot of dark winter days, so there needed to be a public place that was secure, pleasant and well lit."

Positioned over the lobby entrance in the base of the building are square, cast aluminum, custom made fixtures that house cool white fluorescent lamps behind opalescent art glass. The color of the lighting matches the cool light of the metal halides used above. In addition, the fixtures were selected to be cold-weather durable.

The tall bollards situated throughout the outdoor plaza are lit at the top with metal halide multi-vapor lamps. These custom lanterns are made with cast aluminum frames finished with silver metallic paint and gold leafing. The lamp is concealed here also behind art glass, and additionally by an interior diffuser globe made of arcylic to protect the art glass from damage.

"Inexpensive fixtures with acrylic lenses the shape of a mason jar screwed into an aluminum base and fitted with 60-watt incandescent A-lamps are set into the masonry of the granite steps," Johnson explains. "And there's a piece of granite that's an inch and a quarter thick that has a sort of ripple effect over the top of the steps, so we used a red granite to create an enclosure around these generic fixtures set into the steps themselves."

At the planting beds, generic fluorescent fixtures with cold weather ballasts are placed behind skirts of stainless steel, and fastened to the underside of the granite perimeters that also function as benches, allowing them to appear to visually "float."

The 175-watt metal halide uplights at the bases of the trees are turned on all year round. In the winter, they highlight the bare branch structure, and in the summertime, they illuminate the underside of the leaf canopy. For the holidays, the building managers install tiny treelights to create an even more festive atmosphere.

To capitalize on the brisk movement of the water splashing down the fountain's ridges, about 30 submersible pool lights have been installed in a trough at the base of the fountain. In the center of each fountain in the summer, jets shoot up a spray of water in the form of a blue spruce. Four submersible fixtures cast light up into this white frothy water element.

A total of 230 exterior lighting fixtures have been used in this project. Prudential Plaza has received numerous building and lighting awards, including a 1992 IESNA Chicago Section Illumination Design Award, 1991 Chicago Lighting Institute Special Gold Award of Merit, 1991 Brightener Award for near north and downtown Chicago projects, 1991 International Illumination Design Award of Merit from the IESNA, 1990 City Development of the Year Award, and 1990 Best New Building Award.

Two Prudential Plaza's illumination is centered on the north and south sides, which have architecturally interesting 15-foot setbacks.

Project: **One & Two Prudential Plaza**   Location: **Chicago, Illinois**   Architect: **Loebl Schlossman and Hackl, Inc.**   Landscape Architect: **Eric H. Johnson, Loebl Schlossman and Hackl, Inc.**   Lighting Designers: **Eric H. Johnson and Alan H. Larson, Loebl Schlossman and Hackl, Inc.**   Contractors: **Walsh Construction Company of Illinois** *(Two Prudential Plaza)*; and **Pepper Construction Company** *(Outdoor Plaza)*   Electrical Contractor: **Illinois J. Livingston** *(for both buildings and plaza)*
Photographers: **James R. Steinkamp, Steinkamp/Ballogg Photography, Chicago** *(Two Prudential Plaza)*; and **Scott McDonald, Hedrich Blessing** *(Outdoor plaza)*
Lighting Manufacturers: **Prescolite**—*tree uplights*; **Hydrel**—*sidewalk signliters*; **General Electric Lighting**—*multi-vapor HID and fluorescent lamps*; **Cooper Lighting**—*top of building fixtures*; **Philips Lighting**—*multi-vapor HID lamps*

The custom-designed bollards that illuminate the plaza house metal halide lamps and are made with art glass and cast aluminum.

Scott McDonald, Hedrich Blessing

James R. Steinkamp, Steinkamp/Ballogg Photography, Chicago

The old and new Prudential buildings are joined at the mezzanine and lobby levels.

The illumination from multi-vapor metal halide fixtures makes Prudential Plaza a distinctive and easily recognizable landmark in Chicago's skyline.

Submersible pool lights illuminate the play of water as it spashes down the sloped fountain steps.

NEC HEADQUARTERS BUILDING

CRITERIA

The headquarters for NEC, an electronics manufacturer, is a 43-story office building that occupies a full city block in the Mita area of Tokyo. The height of the 180-meter high rocket-shaped skyscraper was influenced by limited space and high traffic levels on the ground. As the construction of the building was being completed, plans for its lighting were being conceived.

The lighting goal was to make the building a distinctive landmark in the nightscape of the city. The challenge for lighting designer, Motoko Ishii, was increased by owner-imposed energy use limitations that complicated the design.

Before the decision was made to highlight the upper portions of the building, Ishii and the design team conducted surveys of the building and its surroundings, including pedestrian views from the Shinkasen (superfast train), commuter trains, monorails, and highways.

Stringent governmental regulations eliminated fixture positions from across the street at ground level, creating an added challenge in the search for a way to provide illumination at the top of the building.

FULFILLMENT

Since installation within or on the structure was not possible either, the bulk of the equipment has been installed on platforms built onto the above-ground plaza and concealed by landscaping. From fixtures mounted in these positions, light is cast directly upward along the smooth walls of the building.

The base of the building intentionally remains in shadow, with the illumination levels increasing towards the top to create the illusion that the upper floors are floating in the sky.

Mrs. Ishii, who often incorporates a sense of changing time in her work, has allowed the NEC to function via the lighting as a timepiece for the inhabitants of Tokyo. Beginning at 8:00 P.M., fixtures fitted with 1.8 kilowatt metal halide and energy-saving xenon lamps are circuited into groups that are turned off one by one at hourly intervals, the successively lighted patterns gradually growing dimmer as they proceed toward the top of the building, until the last group switches off at midnight.

Five lighting systems were mocked up at the site to help determine the final positioning of the fixtures. Finally, groupings of fixtures were installed to the north and south sides of the 1,500 square meter building. Each group includes four 1.8-kilowatt metal halide lamps and seven 1-kilowatt xenon searchlights, two with color filters.

The color of the floodlighting at the top is varied seasonally by changing color filters: light blue in spring and summer, coral in autumn and winter.

This project has received a 1991 International Illumination Design Award, the Paul Waterbury Award of Excellence for Outdoor Lighting for the Illuminating Engineering Society of North America.

Project: **NEC Headquarters Building**   Location: **Tokyo, Japan**   Client: **NEC Corporation**   Architect: **Nikken Sekkei Ltd.**
Lighting Designer: **Motoko Ishii, Motoko Ishii Lighting Design Inc.**   Photographers: **Yoshiro Kato and Motoko Ishii Lighting Design Inc.**

Ground-mounted metal halide and xenon flood-lights illuminate the building energy efficiently.

The changing nighttime lighting shown as it appears between 11:00 p.m. and midnight.

NEW ENGLAND TELEPHONE

CRITERIA

The New England Telephone building is situated behind the Post Office Square Park, and so one of the goals of the renovation was to highlight the 22-story tower's clean-lined Art Deco facade and make it a pleasing backdrop to the park, without overpowering it.

An added challenge was to make the entry more inviting, as well as provide a more interesting streetscape. The bare concrete sidewalks are as much as 30 feet wide, and the building's walls were bare at the first floor. The existing facade also included a 45-foot high air intake louver directly above the entry doors.

FULFILLMENT

The designers chose to illuminate the facade and upper setbacks to accent window strips and stone ornamentation with an interplay of light and shadow. Narrow beam, 400-watt, and 1,000-watt metal halide floodlights are placed above the fifth floor and aimed vertically adjacent to each window strip. Smaller fixtures mounted on window sills highlight strips on the second to fourth floors.

At the entrance, the designers created an illuminated architectural form made of bronze and translucent glass that complements the building's Art Deco style, and includes a canopy and the air intake equipment. Four 175-watt metal halide floodlights shine light up within the 45-foot high lightboxes. The fixtures' positioning at the bottoms of the boxes makes maintenance easy. The units can be fitted with color filters for holidays or special occasions. The horizontal light-boxes are fitted with fluorescents.

New features have been added to the streetscape, including flagpoles, trees, planters and patterned granite sidewalk paving. Adorning the building are striking bronze decorative sconces, each housing one 250-watt incandescent lamp, dimmed 50 percent to extend lamp life. The bronze telephone kiosks are equipped with two, 7-watt compact fluorescent lamps that cast light through the glass roof and onto the telephone within.

Decorative lighting elements have created a nighttime presence for the renovated building.

Project: **New England Telephone Headquarters Building Renovation**   Location: **Boston, Massachusetts**   Client: **New England Telephone Company**
Architect: **Joan E. Goody, FAIA, principal-in-charge, and Gabriel Gualteros, Goody, Clancy & Associates**   Landscape Architect: **The Halvorson Company, Inc.**
Lighting Designer: **Candace M. Kling, C.M. Kling & Associates, Inc.**   Contractor: **Turner Construction Company**   Photographer: **Peter Vanderwarker**
Lighting Manufacturer: **Sterner Lighting**

The sconces are made with bronze and translucent glass.

The streetscape has been planned to tie in with the building, including bronze telephone kiosks.

The added decorative lighting treatment has emphasized and enhanced the building's appearance by day as well.

The New England Telephone building serves as a pleasing backdrop for the Post Office Square Park situated in front of it.

Art Deco style sconces complement the building's architecture.

The bronze sconces each contain one 250-watt incandescent lamp dimmed 50 percent.

Metal halide fixtures illuminate the building's translucent panels.

bioMerieux VITEK, INC.

CRITERIA

The goal of this lighting design was to capitalize on the building's form by night. Since the structure is located near Lambert International Airport and several academic institutions, its nighttime image would be visible to many from miles around.

FULFILLMENT

The band of windows on each floor allows refreshing daylight into the work spaces by day, and at night they establish a visual signature for the building. "Zippers" of glass block that allow natural light into the stairwells, embody the striking nighttime illumination statement at night.

The vertical exterior lighting effect is achieved with 3- and 4-foot-long fluorescent strip fixtures fitted with asymmetrical reflectors positioned along the glass block. The vertical lines of light create a spaceship-like effect.

The exterior lighting complements that of the interior, where general illumination comes from recessed fluorescent energy-saving fixtures, with a modular wiring system for flexibility, as well as incandescent and HID lighting fixtures made with polymeric materials.

The laboratory spaces use recessed parabolic fluorescent fixtures, some with protective plastic sheeting.

Project: **bioMerieux Vitek, Inc.**   Location: **St. Louis, Missouri**   Client: **bioMerieux Vitek, Inc.**   Architect: **Mackey Mitchell Associates**
Lighting Designer: **Mackey Mitchell Associates/WTA Associates Engineers**   Photographer: **Sam Fentress**   Lighting Manufacturers: **Lithonia**

The verticality of the structure is emphasized by the fluorescent lines of light that emanate from concealed fixtures.

INTERSTATE TOWER

CRITERIA

The rocket-ship shaped top of Interstate Tower in Charlotte, North Carolina, is tall enough to be visible from the city's surrounding highways. Lighting designer Craig A. Roeder, IES, IALD, was called in at the beginning of the project to create an image for Interstate Tower by night.

Though the lighting was designed to promote universal identification of the building, Roeder incorporated a playful aspect in his design as well. The lighting is capable of animation and chasing effects that make the top of the tower seem like a rocket ship ready to take off. "It chases for holidays and during festivals held downtown," says Roeder. "And everybody talks about it when they turn the lights on, because it makes it more special."

FULFILLMENT

The globes or metal hemispheres that dot the perimeter of the ledge that borders the bottom of the spaceship-like cylindrical portion of the building are intended to evoke an old-fashioned, almost Deco feeling. The whole globes are decorative; the halved ones contain high-pressure sodium light fixtures.

"I used high-pressure sodium because we found a color corrected lamp that would last well, and went well with the quartz lamps used elsewhere," says Roeder.

Though there are offices in the cylindrical top of the building, the lights don't bother the occupants. "Anytime the light fixtures are aimed straight up on a building, there usually is no problem. It is when the lights are mounted away from the building that there can be problems," says Roeder.

Long-life, 10,000-hour metal halide fixtures were affordable only for mounting on top of the roof. The slope is bathed in light from 70-watt fixtures. Neon is used inside the rails on the roof, as well as in the rings around the cylinder. The pinnacle is illuminated with one 250-watt lamp concealed behind acid-frosted glass. Two PAR 56 fixtures light the top spire. Several 500-watt halogen spot fixtures are used lower on the crown as well.

The 3000 degree Kelvin color temperature of the neon and metal halide lamps makes them color compatible with the halogen fixtures lower on the crown.

The light animation from three rings of chasing halogen PAR 38 strips that flash in varied patterns is accomplished via a programmable controller.

One of the building's windows opens for maintenance access to the fixtures.

Project: **Interstate Tower**   Location: **Charlotte, North Carolina**   Developer: **Faison Associates**
Architect: **Gary Handel, senior associate partner-in-charge, Kohn Pedersen Fox**   Associate Architect: **Steve Thomas and Mike Grabman, Odell Associates, Inc.**
Lighting Designer: **Craig A. Roeder Associates , Inc.**   Engineers: **Randy Ruggles and Dennis Ferguson, King/Guinn Associates** *(structural)*; **Irvin Angel and Virginia Johnson, Benner & Fields** *(mechanical)*; **Connor Builard and Jim Safrit, Bullard Associates** *(electrical)*
Photographer: **Rick Alexander, Rick Alexander & Associates, Inc.**   Lighting Manufacturers: **Litelab, Sterner Lighting, Neotek**

A blending of light sources was used, including strip lights that chase via a programmable controller.

The rocket-ship-topped image of Interstate Tower is aided by the inclusion of decorative metal hemispheres.

FLEET NATIONAL BANK

CRITERIA

While involved in the construction and exterior crown lighting design for a new Fleet National Bank building, Randy Burkett, then with HOK, and now principal of his own firm, was commissioned to design a more ambitious lighting scheme for the stately existing Fleet National Bank building—known as the Industrial National Bank when first constructed—adjacent to it in Providence, Rhode Island.

Other than requesting the lighting not make the building look flat, the client had no preconceived ideas as to what the lighting should look like. "Basically, the concept that evolved was to use classical floodlighting techniques, but to selectively light some surfaces and not others, emphasizing setbacks and creating planes with varied luminances to differentiate them," says Burkett.

FULFILLMENT

"When we first got into this project, we thought that since it is a limestone building, it would be brought out best with metal halide sources," says Burkett, "but when we took samples of the limestone that had chipped off from one of the upper elevations and looked at them under different light sources, the metal halide made them look too cool. So we lighted the building with standard high-pressure sodium (HPS). This warm source rendered the fairly cool limestone a neutral and attractive tone." (Burkett notes that in reality, the building does look a bit warmer than it appears in the photograph).

The high-pressure sodium fixtures have been used in a variety of wattages, depending upon the throw required. The illumination is graduated—falling off before it intensifies again at the next setback, to delineate edges and differentiate planes.

In the couple of instances in which building occupants could see the lights through the windows, the fixtures have been fitted with louvers to prevent visual disturbance.

The building is topped with a glowing beacon, visible from miles away. At the top of the building is a glass-enclosed cupola, inside of which is an old metal exhaust stack no longer in use. Clear mercury lamps have been mounted all around the outside of the stack and behind the glass. The cool color cast from the mercury source is in deliberate contrast to the warmer tones of the HPS exterior illumination.

Though the contractor had been given predetermined aiming points based on calculations to follow during the fixture installation, usually with a large building the final aiming of the fixtures by the lighting designer and assistants is a somewhat time-consuming process. Burkett relates an interesting anecdote involving this.

Inadvertently, the bank had invited local television press to cover the event of the first lighting of the building on the night that Burkett and his associates had planned to aim the fixtures.

The nighttime gathering in the square across the street from the structure consisted of about four dozen people, including television station representatives, historic renovation association representatives, and the bank president. Burkett was worried the building would look terrible lighted with unaimed fixtures, but, he says, "There was no way we could keep the building lighting event from happening, and when they flipped the switch, it looked almost perfect. We ended up doing the aiming later, but it took about 15 percent of the time it normally takes on a large floodlighting job."

Burkett attributes the unexpected perfection of the lighting not only to the contractor, who did an accurate job when installing the fixtures, but to the limestone surface, "which is forgiving and predictable. You couldn't get a more matte surface. When you're dealing with granite, glass, marble and other surfaces that shine, you don't know what to expect. But on a limestone building like this, if you know how to read a computer printout and what the numbers mean, you can estimate what's going to happen," he says.

The historical society in Providence awarded the bank a special historical renovation citation for the lighting.

Project: **Fleet National Bank**   Location: **Providence, Rhode Island**
Client: **Fleet National Bank**   Lighting Designer: **Randy Burkett, at the time of the project with Hellmuth, Obata & Kassabaum, Inc. and now president of Randy Burkett Lighting Design, Inc.**   Photographer: **Courtesy of HOK Photography**
Lighting Manufacturer: **Sterner Lighting**

High-pressure sodium fixtures are placed and aimed to emphasize setbacks and architectural details, rather than create a uniform wash which would have given the building a flatter, uninteresting appearance.

It was during the construction of the shorter new Fleet National Bank building that the lighting for the taller, existing bank building was decided upon.

REGENT COURT

CRITERIA

The Regent Court office building in Dearborn, Michigan, is composed of grid-like vertical and horizontal architectural elements. In contrast, the landscape architect designed for the central court, which the building surrounds, an undulating organic sculpture that integrates grass, granite and brick pavers. Lighting designer, Stefan Graf of Illuminart had to create a lighting design for the courtyard sculpture that would complement its flowing lines and unusual character.

FULFILLMENT

Stefan Graf has selected three different light sources to highlight and add a sense of motion to the court: warm and cool metal halide, and low-voltage incandescent.

Lighting is used to create the illusion of motion on the undulating planes specifically by illuminating the sculpture at night to mimic the sun's movement over the surface of the sculpture.

Five custom bollards were designed in 20-, 16- and 8-foot heights to house concealed 240-watt PAR 56 and 75-watt PAR 36, 12-volt fixtures, with ballasts enclosed in the bases. Specific and geometrically complex aiming angles are accommodated by custom louver covers with blades varying from 32 to 48 degrees for glare control.

Each of the pylons has four dimmed circuits controlled by an electronically timed crossfader, with fade times programmed at seven second intervals to slowly change the light patterns on the rolling "hills." The dimming also extends the incandescent lamp life.

The court's perimeter is delineated with low-wattage metal halide 3000 degree Kelvin fixtures. The trees are uplighted with cooler, 4100 degree Kelvin, 175-watt R-lamp metal halide units.

An astronomical time clock controls the court lighting system throughout the year.

Six bollards in varying heights—from a maximum of 10 feet, to a minimum of 4 feet—illuminate the driveway that leads into the courtyard. The graduated height was specified because, though the office building is level, the driveway slopes up, "and we wanted to complement the lines of the building facade," says Graf. "These bollards have a 100-watt metal halide roadway lighting component in them, as well as a 100-watt metal halide uplight in the back of the bollard to wash the building facade, and a small, translucent Plexiglas glow top that houses a 100-watt mercury vapor lamp."

Exterior of Regent Court looking down the motor court

Project: **Regent Court**   Location: **Dearborn, Michigan**   Client: **Ford Motor Land Development**   Architect: **Neumann Smith & Associates**
Landscape Architect: **John Grissim Associates**   Lighting Designer: **Stefan Graf, Illuminart**   Photographer: **Gary Quesada/ B. Korab Ltd.**
Lighting Manufacturers: **GE Lighting, Osram Sylvania, Spaulding, Devine Lighting, Greenlee Lighting, Kim Lighting**

The driveway bollards are installed in varied heights because the driveway slopes.

The driveway bollards are equipped with fixtures that light the roadway and wash the facade of the building.

All of the court lighting is controlled by an astronomical time clock.

The driveway bollards range in height from 10 to 4 feet.

The bollards house metal halide and mercury vapor lamps.

The sculpture is made of grass, granite and brick pavers.

The design of the custom louvers and aiming angles was geometrically complex.

The lights crossfade at a rate of about 7 seconds.

The trees are uplit with 175-watt metal halide lamps.

HOSPITALITY
AND RETAIL

Not all hotels are alike, and consequently, neither is the lighting for them. In this chapter, there are two contrasting examples of how the exterior lighting can be approached. Bally's Park Place in Atlantic City needed glitz to compete with the high-excitement images of its neighbors, and to reflect the expected feeling of excitement associated with the boardwalk city. Kinetic, multi-colored lights mounted behind the tinted glass walls of the hotel, and invisible by day, prove an effective solution. On the other hand, at the Palace of the Lost City located in the quiet midst of a South African desert, the lighting techniques are used to enhance the regal ornateness of the architecture and to create the illusion of a historic past, even though the resort hotel is new.

Retailers welcome the opportunity to lengthen shopping time by attracting customers during nighttime hours, and lighting plays an important role in insuring the shopper's safety and comfort, as well as helping to provide an entertaining and festive atmosphere conducive to making purchases. The well-lit Crossroads Mall relies heavily on burial units that, if touched, can't harm children's curious hands. Preston Center East is proof that a lighting facelift need not be expensive to be effective. And at Bowden Square, the renovation included illuminating the refurbished mansion, that serves as a country club, with the elegance and sense of drama that it deserves.

The concept of building facade as billboard is utilized at Potomac Mills, where backlit plexiglass panels never fail to call passing motorists' attention to the mall, and at Hypermart USA, where giant concrete bollards uniformly illuminate the store's name and signature graphics proudly displayed on the facade.

Included here also are examples in which the playing up of architectural details with light have created attractive, welcoming images for retailers. Note the highlighting of window-like openings at Lazarus Department Store, the 40-foot-high gateway outlined with light at Grossmont Center, and the emphasizing of curves and textured stucco at Harris Department Store.

PALACE OF THE LOST CITY

CRITERIA

Though its ornate architectural details and gold-leafed beauty make it worthy to be a home to royalty, the Palace of the Lost City is not really a palace, but a 352-room luxury hotel accessible to any well-heeled commoner after a two-hour drive northwest of Johannesburg.

The Palace is part of a water park and resort complex envisioned by its owner, Sol Kerzner of Sun International, and designed by architects Wimberly Allison Tong & Goo (WATG). Lighting consultant John Watson, John Watson Landscape Illumination, Inc., was engaged to create the soft landscape lighting; and Craig Roberts, Craig Roberts Lighting Design, was commissioned to complete the interior lighting design, but the exterior building lighting fell to Ross De Alessi, IALD, MIES, Ross De Alessi Lighting Design.

In discussing the project with the architects, De Alessi formed lighting goals focused around several concepts. "The central idea was to create an historic character for the building and the illusion that the Palace was deeply rooted in the ancient culture of the surrounding locale," says De Alessi.

At the same time, the Palace was not to be lit like a cold, uninhabited monument. "A lot of guests arrive in the middle of the night. We wanted it to look like somebody's always home, and waiting for the guest's arrival. We wanted to create the illusion that people lived even in the unoccupied parts of the building, like the towers," De Alessi explains.

FULFILLMENT

Driving toward the Palace, guests first notice the towers in the distance, which are capped by open air domes formed of detailed copper patinated palm fronds.

The tallest tower, adorned by a deer-like kudu frozen in mid-leap at each corner, is the King's Tower, which is also distinguished by a genuine flame burning within its dome. To enhance the effect of the burning torch by giving it a "sense of place" in the darkness, and to balance this dome visually with the other, solely electrically lit tower domes, the large bowl that contains the flame has been uplit with MR 16s.

Because of this tower's great height, its exterior walls have been lit differently from those of the other towers. Asymmetric, 120-volt quartz 350/500-watt floodlights have been used with transformers that provide the needed lumen output within the energy constraints.

"Each of the other tower domes has four quartz floodlights, 300 watts each, and radically dimmed 60 percent to emulate a flame color, that washes up inside the patina of the green leaves to indicate figuratively that 'somebody's home,'" says De Alessi. Tinted compact fluorescent wall packs supplement color and also serve as safety lights.

The exterior walls of these towers are lit with 300-watt quartz floodlights. "The floodlight is positioned against the tower wall so that it bounces light off a reflector built into the balustrade and back onto the wall to create a soft glow, rather than a harsh uplit look," says De Alessi. "The deck behind the balustrade also glows and creates the illusion that there's a burning brazier out on the deck, accompanied by guests enjoying the night air, even though those decks are really uninhabited."

The internally lit domes and the externally glowing walls are controlled separately to reach to 100 percent brightness at dusk, and dim to 60 percent over one hour. Most of the control switches are housed in each of the towers.

The low-set, enclosed Rotunda dome is illuminated with a multi-tiered system. The base is ringed with 1500 mm cool-white fluorescent lamps in lensed uplight fixtures that flatter the patinated color of the large leaves. The central portion is lit by roof-mounted, dimmed PAR 56 heads outfitted with snoots and louvers. The finial is lit with two 12-volt, 5-degree pinspots. The lions on either side of the dome are uplit with lensed, louvered and snooted MR 16s. All the fixtures are positioned so that they are concealed from the view of guests, whose rooms surround the Rotunda.

The kudu fountain in front of the Rotunda has graceful arches of water shooting inward from the horns of the animals. The water is illuminated a bright white by non-filtered, submersible niche-mounted MR 16s with linear spread lenses. De Alessi notes that "with South Africa's 240-volt, 50 Hz line voltage, filament sizes of lamps must be quite large, so employing the 12-volt MR 16 fixtures is a must for critical focal lighting, with their small filaments and great beam control."

The East Gate Bridge leads to an open court in which a bronze replica of the great elephant Shawu is displayed center stage. The elephant sculpture is highlighted with shielded PAR 56 very narrow spot fixtures fitted with long-barrel snoots and louvers, and concealed high in the towers. In the Elephant Court, two genuine gas torches have been added to soften the effect of steep focal lighting.

The Cheetah fountain greets guests as they round the entry's driveway and glide into the porte cochere. The sculptures, depicting cheetahs and impalas in 1⅓ scale, are colorfully sidelit by waterproof MR 16 fixtures fitted with glass diffusion and color filters, that are submersed in the fountain. Leopards, the symbol of Bophuthatswana, top the porte cochere and are crosslit with frosted lensed and snooted MR 16s, as are most of the building sculptures, to enhance the three-dimensional qualities and separate them from the background.

The exterior walls of the towers are lit with 300-watt quartz floodlights.

Project: **Palace of the Lost City**   Location: **Republic of Bophuthatswana, South African Homeland**   Owner: **Sol Kerzner, Dene Murphy; project manager, Sun International**
Design Architect: **Gerald L. Allison, Eduardo Robles, Bobby Caragay, Wimberly Allison Tong & Goo (WATG)**   Architect of Record: **Tony Doherty, Burg Doherty Bryant & Partners**
Project Manager: **Rod Oosthuizen, Charles Israelite, Colin Rothschild, Schneid Israelite & Partners**   Lighting Designer *(exterior and hard landscape)*: **Ross De Alessi, IALD, MIES,**
Ross De Alessi Lighting   Lighting Designer *(soft landscape)*: **John Watson, John Watson Landscape Illumination, Inc.**   Lighting Designer *(interiors)*: **Craig Roberts,**
Craig Roberts Lighting Design   Interior Designer: **Trisha Wilson, James Cary, Wilson & Associates**   Electrical Engineer: **Jose Granado, Biderman Finn Beekhuizen**
Sculptor: **Dahie De Jager**   Photographer: **Ross De Alessi**   Lighting Manufacturers: **GE Lighting, Tungsram, Osram Sylvania**—*lamps*; **Hydrel**—*underwater and fountain fixtures*;
Elliptipar Inc.—*asymmetric fixtures*; **Lascon**—*PAR-holders, floodlights, and roadway luminaries*

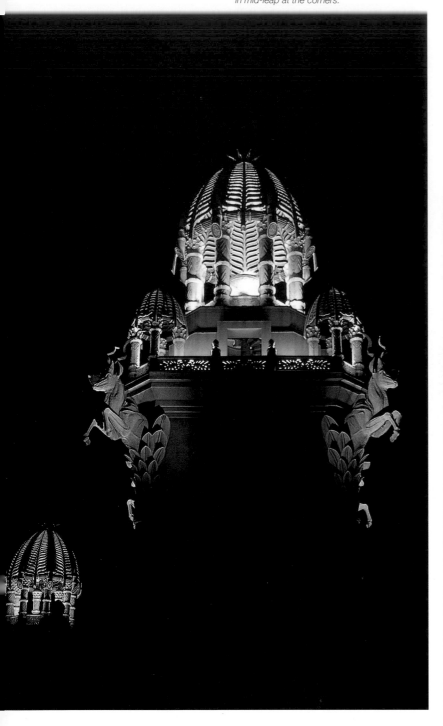

The King's Tower, the tallest tower, is marked also by an ever-burning flame and kudus frozen in mid-leap at the corners.

The gold-leafed Cheetah fountain is uplit with submerged PAR 38 fixtures that crosslight the sculptured elements.

The exterior of the lobby lounge area, adjacent to the pool, is uplit with dimmed 30-watt, PAR 56 narrow spot submersible fixtures. The cables are dressed and the fixtures concealed here, as in other outdoor areas, in rockwork and precast elements, so as not to be conspicuous in the daytime.

The pool bar pavilions are uplit with sconces that use A-lamps and PAR 38s. The decorative portion of the sconces have been designed by Trisha Wilson, and the fixture "guts" have been designed by De Alessi and Leif Johnson, who is with Luminae Souter.

Combinations of 80-, 120- and 150-watt quartz PAR, and incandescent PAR 38s are used extensively in burial and surface-mounted uplights to highlight tall columns. The multi-tiered decorative ornamentation in the columns has been designed specifically to hold light fixtures. Archways are highlighted with PAR 38s and 56s, in various wattages ranging from 60 to 300 watts.

The Rotunda's enclosed dome is uplit with MR 16s. The fountain is lit with submersed fixtures.

To illuminate pathways, custom bollards have been installed that use 26-watt compact fluorescent lamps and are heavily shielded, so as not to detract from the vision of the Palace. Sharp cut-off, 70-150-watt, deluxe high-pressure sodium custom luminaires light the roadways.

Regarding energy efficiency, De Alessi explains, "In any design that I do, I always consider energy conservation. In this project, because it's located in the desert, and it's expensive to bring power out there, I used compact fluorescents where I could—for example, in the bollards, the stairwells, and the tower domes. And the roadway lighting fixtures use energy-efficient, deluxe high-pressure sodium (HPS)." The quartz PAR and halogen infrared T lamps also are dimmed to increase lamp life and conserve energy.

"We transformed voltage from 240 to 120 in certain places to use the halogen infrared (HIR) technology lamps. From there we also stepped down for 12 volt," says De Alessi. "Though there are no outstanding import limits, the import duties are hefty, especially when there's glass involved. So we used a minimum of American equipment—some sophisticated asymmetric and fountain lightng fixtures, but mostly we modified South African PAR and fluorescent lampholders."

Custom accessories had to be designed for local equipment to accommodate the special colored and spread lenses. "Leif Johnson gets 90 percent of the credit for designing the accessories," says De Alessi. In fact, the South African manufacturer, Lascon, has cataloged many of the items.

In addition to a 1992 IALD Award of Excellence this project is a Semi-Finalist in the GE Lighting Edison Award competition.

Shawu the Elephant is crosslit with roof-mounted fixtures positioned to be as unobtrusive by day as possible.

The abundance of nighttime illumination is intended to make the arriving guest feel as if someone is always up and about in the Palace.

Architects at WATG created the ornate and opulent vision of the Palace by day.

Even the animal sculptures mounted on the Palace are crosslit to create a sense of drama.

The Palace of the Lost City is a new luxury resort deliberately illuminated at night to appear ancient and historical in character.

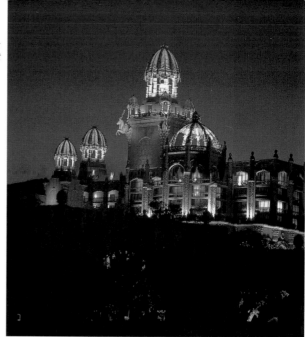

Fixtures are concealed in multi-leveled capitals. Towers are vignetted with soft brushes of light.

OLD OAKS COUNTRY CLUB

CRITERIA

The Old Oaks Country Club in Purchase, New York, is housed in a former private mansion in a wealthy area of the city. The architect was hired to renovate the building facade, which had begun to deteriorate from age and weather conditions. Lighting designer Robert Singer was commissioned to provide lighting not only for the facade, but the entire site, which included roadways, parking lots and landscaping.

Previously, the building had been floodlit, but rendered in a flat and uninteresting way. Though there were budgetary constraints for the renovation, the owner's goal was that the architecture of the building be enhanced, and a dramatic, elegant environment be established for their dues-paying members.

FULFILLMENT

Durable, virtually maintenance-free fiberglass has been used on the facade to replace the deteriorating plaster. The approach taken by Singer was to highlight the ornate, graceful architecture with an interplay of light and dark areas. "With a facade like this, it's not necessary to floodlight the whole building," says Singer. "Instead, elements important to the architecture can be emphasized with light, making for a much more dramatic presentation."

Generally, the lighting is accomplished with ground-mounted fixtures that cast light all the way up to the top of the columns. "There's about a 60-80 foot throw with some of these fixtures," says Singer. "We were originally going to use high-intensity discharge units, but they weren't cost-effective, so 90-watt quartz PAR 38 fixtures have been specified. They come in spot and flood types, but, in most cases, we used spots."

Positioning some of the fixtures behind the columns creates a sense of depth and dimension. At the front of the building, the smaller columns on top and in front of the porte cochere are highlighted with PAR 30 fixtures; the larger columns are uplighted with 90-watt PAR 38s.

The lanterns at the front entrance, which had existed previously, have been cleaned, refinished and restored. Patterned rays emanate from the light of 100-watt, A-19 lamps cast through pebble-glass panels. A large chandelier, which had been suspended at the front entrance, has been relocated to the side of the building.

Submerged incandescent fixtures fitted with rich blue glass filters illuminate the water in the fountain at the front entrance. The fountain sculptures are accented with uplight from 250-watt, very narrow spot PAR 38 fixtures.

In the rotunda at the rear of the building, a combination of PAR 30 and adjustable MR 16 fixtures are used.

To preserve the integrity of the design and for ease of maintenance, individual circuits have been connected to timers, which turn the lights on when needed.

Project: **Old Oaks Country Club**　　　Location: **Purchase, New York**　　　Client: **Old Oaks Country Club**　　　Architect: **Bruce Levy, Hastings Design Group**
Lighting Designer: **Robert Singer, Robert Singer and Associates**　　　Photographer: **Robert H. Singer**
Lighting Manufacturers: **York, Bronzelite, GE Lighting, Kim Lighting**

Smaller columns on the top level and in front of the porte cochere are highlighted with PAR 30 fixtures.

Ground-mounted fixtures cast illumination up to the top of the lower-level columns.

The Old Oaks Country Club is housed in a former private mansion.

Positioning some fixtures behind columns creates a sense of depth and dimension.

Patterned rays emanate from the light of 100-watt A-19 lamps cast through pebble glass.

Drama is created by the intentional interplay of light and shadow.

BALLY'S PARK PLACE

CRITERIA

The lighting designers Allan Leibow and Donald Gersztoff, WGFS, were charged with creating an exciting and flexible nighttime image for Bally's Park Place Casino Hotel in Atlantic City, New Jersey, that would be easy to maintain.

FULFILLMENT

The exterior lighting for the hotel is actually mounted inside the hotel. By day, the incandescent fixtures are concealed from view by the curtain wall of reflective glass. At night, the fixtures are mounted on a slab concealed in a banquette in each guest room, and the light is visible through the glass curtain wall of the building.

The color theme of Bally's—magenta and white—is embodied in the fixtures. Each fixture contains two clear, 150-watt incandescent lamps. One side of the fixture has a clear glass lens to show white light, and the other side is fitted with a magenta lens. Large facets on the reflectors around the lamp allow the filament to be reflected at several angles, creating sparkle.

These 120-volt lamps are run on 70 volts of power, saving energy, increasing lamp life to 60 times the manufacturer's rating, and easing maintenance by cutting down on the number of required lamp changes.

Lamps are controlled in groups of six (three fixtures), with 24 lamps per circuit. The group circuiting substantially reduced the dimming system cost.

The basic program adds a new pattern to the building every 30 seconds. The owners do have the option of programming any pattern they choose at any time. During the Christmas season, for example, a festive pattern of a white Christmas tree with a background of red lamps was displayed.

The light fixtures are actually mounted inside the hotel to produce patterns visible outside the glass curtain wall.

Project: **Bally's Park Place Casino Hotel**   Location: **Atlantic City, New Jersey**   Owner: **Bally's Park Place Casino Hotel**
Owner's Representative/Design Director: **Nicholas Fasciano**   Architect: **David Dann, William B. Tabler Architects**   Lighting Designers: **Donald Gersztoff and Allan Leibow,**
Wheel Gersztoff Friedman Shankar Inc. Lighting Designers   Engineer: **Imre Braun and Don Durang, Lehr Associates**   Photographer: **Allan Leibow**
Lighting Manufacturers: **Illuminating Concepts & Engineering**—*custom fixtures*

BOWDEN SQUARE

CRITERIA

When restaurateur Michael "Buzzy" O'Keefe took over this wooded dining spot, he realized that the previously unilluminated site off a major highway would attract more clientele—specifically, a conservative, older set interested in fine dining, and a younger crowd for the tavern—if it were lit at night. O'Keefe commissioned lighting designer Robert Singer to create a pleasing illuminated garden setting at night, and also to insure that the fascia of the main building of Bowden Square could be noticed through the landscaping by passing motorists.

A major restriction was that the lighting had to be designed and installed in five days—in time for the Fourth of July weekend—for under $5,000. "The owner had a definite idea of the type of lighting he wanted," says Singer, "which helped get the job done on time." The owner wanted the garden and landscape to have a magical look, to create an extraordinary setting in which clients could relax and enjoy a drink, or have dinner in the outdoor patio, surrounded by natural beauty.

FULFILLMENT

The landscaping contained vibrant bursts of color from trees such as Colorado Blue Spruce and Japanese Red Maple, and other flora and fauna. To play up the colorful beauty, Singer specified dichroic lamps in ground-mounted fixtures.

"With dichroics, since the filters are within the lamps, and not serving as a lens, only a pure, true color is emitted," says Singer. "This provides more visual punch, rather than just a diffusion of color." The reinforced color from the lighting adds the sense of fun and magic for which the owner was looking.

Specifically, 150-watt, PAR 38 dichroic floodlights are used to broadly wash the maples with red light, and the spruce trees and shrubbery with blue. Where the blue and red beams intersect, a mystical purple glow is cast.

To produce an ethereal moonlighting effect, a 90-watt very narrow spot backlights the blue spruce. All the fixtures have been ground-mounted at 45-degree angles.

"The ground-mounting was unusual in the case of the moonlighting," says Singer, "because most moonlighting effects are accomplished with fixtures mounted within the tree itself. But this technique provided the best washes, while filtering the light through all the branch layers as well. I used the trees as decorative elements. Instead of lighting them from within, I treated them as if they were part of a stage set."

Ground-mounted fixtures, Singer notes, are also easier to maintain than tree-mounted units. "You don't have to climb the trees or use ladders to replace the lamps," he says. "In many cases, after the initial installation, that effort is not made to relamp the fixtures by the client, and so a really beautiful landscape exists for six months, and then it's history. Simple relamping procedures are crucial to any project."

Ground-mounting also eliminated unsightly wiring on tree trunks and allowed for clean ground burial of all wiring. "You don't want to see the light sources—you want to see what the sources do," says Singer.

The visible tulip and mushroom shaped decorative fixtures used to delineate the garden area house 40-watt A lamps that cast 6-foot pools of light into the patio. The mushroom lamps are spaced 12 feet on center to illuminate pathways for patrons who want to explore the gardens and stroll to the tavern at the other end of Bowden Square.

The main building and tavern exteriors are illuminated with incandescent washes from 150-watt PAR 38 lamps. Initially, low-voltage sources had been in place on the property, but they didn't offer enough illumination to draw people in.

Singer initially installed the fixtures in Bowden Square temporarily to meet the stringent holiday weekend deadline. The following summer, they were permanently installed.

Project: **Bowden Square**   Location: **Southampton, New York**
Client: **Michael "Buzzy" O'Keefe**
Lighting Designer: **Robert Singer, Robert Singer & Associates, Inc.**
Landscape Architect: **Michael "Buzzy" O'Keefe**   Electrician: **Robert Singer**
Photographer: **Robert H. Singer**   Lighting Manufacturers: **GE Lighting, Kim Lighting**

The owner wanted striking illumination to cause passing motorists to take notice.

Ground-mounted fixtures project light up into the layers of leaves.

The Colorado Blue Spruce is front-lit with a dichroic blue filtered lamp and from behind with a 90-watt very narrow spot.

Visible decorative fixtures are used on walkways to provide patrons with a sense of safety and to encourage them to explore the garden.

The use of solely ground-mounted fixtures eliminates the need for ladders and tree-climbing to relamp.

Incandescent building facade lighting draws the motorists' eyes back from the landscaping to the restaurant and tavern.

The natural colorations of the varied landscaping are played up by the dichroic lamps.

PRESTON CENTER EAST

CRITERIA

Lighting designer Craig A. Roeder, IES, IALD, says of the renovation of the Preston Center East shopping complex in Dallas, Texas, "It's a low-budget project, but it shows that with a few lights, you can work wonders." Though the project involved giving the shopping center a significant facelift, in comparison to other costs, the new lighting was relatively inexpensive.

FULFILLMENT

Quartz-lamped burial units dimmed slightly, which helps extend lamp life, and mounted flush with the ground are positioned to cast uplight onto the tall towers. Decorative, wall-mounted sconces cast uplight and downlight, adding sprays of light to the walls between the window displays. Both forms of lighting enhance the rough texture of the walls by grazing them and incorporating interesting highlights into the look of the monotone white facades.

The glass pyramids that top the towers like beacons in the four city block shopping center are made with greenhouse, acid-etched glass panels backlit with fluorescents. The cold cathode backlighting of some of the store's signage makes it seem to float off the facade.

The festive atmosphere of the shopping center is extended onto the sidewalks and into the parking lots via the lighting fixtures concealed in the trees. The live oaks retain their leaves year-round, and so each night dappled patterns of light are cast on the ground, assuring shoppers of the safety of the surrounding environment in an aesthetically pleasing way.

Acid-etched glass-paneled and metal-framed
pyramids backlit with fluorescents top the towers.

Project: **Preston Center East**   Location: **Dallas, Texas**
Developer: **Kenneth H. Hughes Interests**
Architect: **Dale Selzer and Mark Reuschle, Selzer Associates Inc.**
Lighting Designer: **Craig A. Roeder Associates , Inc.**   Photographer: **Robert A. Cook**
Lighting Manufacturers: **Hydrel, Neotek, Hubbell Lighting**

Tower facades are illuminated with quartz burial units.

Light fixtures hidden in the trees cast dappled patterns onto the ground in the adjacent parking spaces.

POTOMAC MILLS

CRITERIA

This large manufacturers' outlet mall is over one mile long. The main entrance was to be representative of the scale of the large mall in its high visibility and prominence. The developers also wanted it to embody an industrial warehouse/factory style.

FULFILLMENT

The original architectural intent had been to use white-painted metal panels on the facade between the large columns. Lighting designer Stefan Graf discussed the exterior concept with the architects and it was decided that instead of using metal panels, translucent plexiglass panels would be a better choice. Backlit, the plexiglass would transform the facade into a luminous billboard visible from the roadway, and reflecting light out into the parking area for shoppers' safety and comfort as well.

Positioned behind the panels are metal halide uplights and downlights that cast light onto the panels, and down onto the walkway. On top of each column, an industrial sportslighter unit has been specified to shine light down the columns and further light the walkway in front of the entrance.

Potomac Mills is a large scale manufacturers'
warehouse outlet mall with a grand entrance to
match its over a mile long presence.

Project: **Potomac Mills**   Location: **Fairfax, Virginia**
Client: **Western Development Corporation**   Architect: **Wah Yee Associates**
Lighting Designer: **Stefan Graf**   Photographer: **Stefan Graf, Illuminart**
Lighting Manufacturers: **Abolite, Capri Lighting, Hubbell, Litelab, Altman, Spaulding, Lithonia, Microreflector, Electro Controls, ARC Sales**

Plexiglass panels backlit with metal halide fixtures create a billboard effect visible to passing motorists on the nearby roadway.

HARRIS DEPARTMENT STORE

CRITERIA

The client wanted its new Moreno Valley, California, department store to embody a youthful and friendly, but sophisticated image. The design team at Space Design International (SDI) used color, texture and scale to create a building that complements the architecture of the surrounding area and the Towngate Shopping Center, and fits in with its semi-desert location 90 miles east of Los Angeles.

The sandy-toned stucco facade is punctuated by the entranceway's curved surface covered with a grid of green slate. The lighting design had to enhance the architecture and identify the store to mall visitors and passing motorists by night.

FULFILLMENT

The 175-watt metal halide uplights mounted to the building exterior graze the textured stucco with light. The building is topped with 40-watt fluorescent uplights. In addition, 40-watt fluorescent uplights create a clean line of light that runs across the top of the facade.

The curved entranceway is emphasized and a sense of dimension is created by light emanating from concealed 40-watt fluorescent fixtures mounted vertically behind the edges of the curved facade. Attention is attracted to merchandise in store windows by a combination of track-mounted, line-voltage, 75-watt, halogen PAR lamps and track-mounted, 25-watt low-voltage accent lights.

Note how close the computer rendering has come to the actual look of the building.

Computer technology was used to design the building and the exterior lighting. Here's the CADD output of the building by day.

Project: **Harris Department Store**   Location: **Moreno Valley, California**
Client: **The Harris Company**
Architect: **Brian Cornelius, Space Design International, Cincinnati, Ohio**
Lighting Designer: **David Apfel, Space Design International, New York, New York**
Contractor: **Ken O'Dell, Magnum Enterprises Inc.**   Photographer: **Paul Bielenberg**

Illumination from concealed, vertically mounted fluorescent fixtures visually draws the entrance facade away from the rest of the building.

This CADD computer generated rendering shows what the lighting was to look like by night.

GROSSMONT CENTER

CRITERIA

To keep up with its competition, the owners of Grossmont Center in La Mesa, California, wanted the renovation to provide a stronger, more identifiable image for the open-air mall. The design team at Space Design International (SDI) designed a striking 40-foot-high gateway to mark the entrance, integrating a glass canopy, an arch and a large brass medallion bearing the mall's new logo. The archway, glass canopy and logo are design elements repeated throughout the mall to give it a unified and fresh image. Lighting had to be incorporated into the gateway to extend the striking image into the night.

FULFILLMENT

Flanking the entrance are a pair of large and long custom-designed, 40-watt lanterns fitted with fluorescent lamps that serve both as functional and decorative elements.

The architectural detailing of the gateway is defined via a series of 150-watt metal halide uplights that are hidden in the setbacks of the gate. The inside of the arch is bathed in the warm glow from 150-watt, high-pressure sodium uplights.

Touches of color—red neon encircling the top of the structure, and yellow banding the lower side setbacks—complete the added interest that lighting can give to an architecturally articulated structure.

Design elements used in the entryway are repeated throughout the mall to establish a sense of unity.

Project: **Grossmont Center**   Location: **La Mesa, California**
Client: **The Grossmont Shopping Center**
Architect: **Doug Meyer, Space Design International, Calabasas, California**
Landscape Architect: **Clay Perdue, Garner Perdue Associates**
Lighting Designer: **Babu Shankar, Wheel Gersztoff Friedman Shankar Associates**
Contractor: **Dean Ninteman, Ninteman Construction**   Photographer: **Paul Bielenberg**

Large decorative sconces containing fluorescent lamps flank the sides of the gateway.

LAZARUS DEPARTMENT STORE

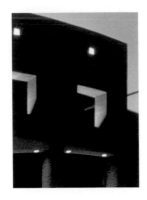

CRITERIA

This prototype store for the Lazarus Department Store chain included an architecturally interesting entrance facade, filled with carefully thought out detail and dimension. Stefan Graf of Illuminart had designed the interior lighting for the store, and so when it came to developing a concept for the exterior, his further involvement was a natural outgrowth.

Because of the unusual architecture, Graf wanted to do more than flat floodlight the exterior, and the client agreed.

FULFILLMENT

The earth-toned facade is complemented by the yellow glow of 35-watt high-pressure sodium fixtures placed to highlight the facade's interesting features. Floodlights have been mounted, for example, behind the square, window-like openings to uplight them. The 20-degree, high-pressure sodium uplights mounted in the corners accent the vertical height of the structure. And 35-watt high-pressure sodium rectangular, recessed step-lights are mounted in the sides of the architectural "bumpouts" to create pools of light. The louvers fitted on those fixtures cast light back onto the wall to accent the corners.

High-pressure sodium floodlights also wash the sides of the building that bound the entranceway.

Recessed, adjustable PAR 36 10-degree spotlights placed at the top of the vertical columns and in the archway cast light down the side of the columns. These spotlights are circuited to a dimmer and set to operate at 80 percent to extend lamp life. The points of light at the top of the building are created by an 8,000 hour sign lamp recessed 4 inches inside the brick to create the glow.

In contrast to the warm high-pressure sodium and incandescent fixtures, the "people lighting" in the walkways comes from bollards that house cool 100-watt metal halide lamps. Metal halide fixtures are also used over and in the entrance vestibule.

This store has been designed as a prototype for the Lazarus Department Store chain.

Project: **Lazarus Department Store**   Location: **Kenwood Mall, Cincinnati, Ohio**   Client: **Lazarus Department Store**   Architect & Landscape Architect: **Baxter, Hodell, Donnelley & Preston**   Interior Designer: **Space Design International**   Lighting Designer: **Stefan Graf, Illuminart**   Contractor: **Stephen Gross & Sons Construction Company**
Photographer: **© Wayne Cable, Cable Studios, Inc.**   Lighting Manufacturers: **Osram Sylvania, Devine Lighting, Hadco, Hubbell, Kirlin Company**

The warm glow of high-pressure sodium fixtures on the building is contrasted by the cool, bluish light from metal halide lamps housed in the walkway bollards.

High-pressure sodium fixtures are carefully placed to highlight the dimension and warm earth tones of the exterior.

HYPERMART USA

CRITERIA

Wal-Mart Stores wanted the exterior lighting of the 222,500 square foot discount/grocery store, Hypermart USA in Topeka, Kansas, to enhance the facade's visual appeal, while minimizing electrical costs. The client did not want light fixtures installed that would obstruct the view of the store's bold red signage. The lighting design for the facade also had to complement the illumination in the adjacent parking lot.

FULFILLMENT

The designers chose to use light to transform the facade into a giant billboard. Heavy duty bollards made of glazed concrete block to stand up to contact with shopping carts and delivery trucks sans damage have been placed in the center section of the building to highlight the Hypermart sign.

The uniformly spaced bollards are tiled in blue to match the band of blue on the facade and the blue delivery doors. The units are fitted with 400-watt metal halide lamps, which is a long-lived and energy-efficient source. Since metal halide is also the light source used in the parking lot, there is no jarring transition in color.

Exterior screen walls, on both sides of the center section, are lighted with 175-watt metal halide lamps. The ribbed barrel vaults in the entrances are uplit with concealed 250-watt metal halide fixtures positioned at the bases and add to the striking exterior image of the building by night. The client, pleased with the results, has used the same exterior lighting techniques in other Hypermarts nationwide.

The curving vaults are uplit with concealed metal halide fixtures.

Project: **Hypermart USA**   Location: **Topeka, Kansas**
Client: **Wal-Mart Stores, Inc.; Douglas Bryant, senior staff architect and Mark Endecott, staff architect**   Architect: **BSW Architects**
Lighting Designer: **Larsen Engineering, Inc.**
Electrical Engineer: **John D. Truskett, P.E., principal, JT/A, Inc.**
Photographer: © **John B. Petersen, John B. Petersen Photography, Inc. Tulsa, OK**
Lighting Manufacturers: **Holophane Co., Inc., Osram Sylvania, Sterner Lighting**

Concrete bollards that house metal halide lamps illuminate the bold signage without obstructing its view.

CROSSROADS MALL

CRITERIA

Lighting designer Craig A. Roeder, IES, IALD was called in early on this project—the renovation of an addition to the Crossroads Mall shopping center in San Antonio, Texas. There is a riverwalk in San Antonio and though this mall is not on it, the architect wanted to promote the feeling that it was part of that kind of lush and relaxing natural environment.

FULFILLMENT

Most of the lighting, which involves highlighting the architectural columns, is accomplished with burial units fitted with a quartz light source. "They are designed with double glass tops, so if children in this very public place touch them they won't get burned," says Roeder. The double glass prevents the glass within reach from becoming too hot.

The fountain in the water feature is illuminated with 1000-watt quartz fixtures. The pathway encircling the large pool is lit with steplights that contain energy-efficient PL compact fluorescent lamps. The arm-mounted metal uplight sconces on the columns emit a warm glow from standard A-lamps.

The underside of the exterior atrium roof is uplit from ground-mounted 250-watt quartz spotlights. The glass-walled atrium is brightened by accent lighting clearly visible to shoppers enjoying the outdoors and contributing to the safe, festive and comfortable mall atmosphere.

The sparkling tree lights, a simple touch, but effective in creating visual interest and excitement, are kept on year-round.

Project: **Crossroads Mall**   Location: **San Antonio, Texas**
Architect: **RTKL-Dallas**
Lighting Designer: **Craig A. Roeder Associates, Inc.**
Photographer: **© 1993 Mark Segal, Chicago**
Lighting Manufacturers: **Hydrel, Sterner, Litelab, Norbert Belfer Lighting**

Burial units are topped with double layers of glass so that inquisitive children will never burn their hands.

LIGHT AND MOTION

The development of sophisticated computer control systems has made possible the creation of light shows. Featured here is the Prometheus Fountain—a light show that mixes changing colors and intensities of light with the ever varying motion of frothing, bubbling water.

Light and motion, in the hands of skilled lighting designers, have also transformed unattractive city eyesores into beautiful sculptures. The Oslo Tower is now a pleasing calendar for urban Norwegians, and the visual/audio Tokio monument in Little Edo is a soothing sight for many Japanese commuters.

The American's Sky Sculpture and Lightscape '89 are both multi-media, site-specific extravaganzas enjoyed by thousands that could only be carried off under the expert guidance of an artist/genius with the help of hundreds of volunteers.

The thrilling and precise beauty of laser light is explored in Laser Art Performances and Gifu Memorial, an art form destined, perhaps, to be more widespread as we approach the twenty-first century.

PROMETHEUS FOUNTAIN

CRITERIA

The gold-leafed Prometheus sculpture, created by Paul Manship, and surrounding fountain has been a popular attraction admired by visitors to Rockefeller Center since its installation in January 1934. The larger-than-life, 18-foot-high sculpture, set in a rectangular pool marked by arched sprays of water springing up on either side, went unilluminated until 1958, when it was lit with an array of soft pastel colors by lighting pioneer Abe Feder, Lighting By Feder.

To enhance this first illumination effort, a water wall was added behind the sculpture, and a 12-minute light and water show was devised. Theatrical dimmers were used that controlled the sequence with timers. A row of lights on the perimeter glowed at Prometheus. This marked the first time 500-watt, PAR 64 lamps had been used in this type of application.

Over the years, deterioration from weather and natural wear and tear on fixtures left the fountain in need of a major upgrade. The "umbrella of light" created for Rockefeller Center's GE Building (formerly the RCA Building), Promenade, Channel Gardens and Lower Plaza by Abe Feder in the 1980s upstaged the Prometheus Fountain as well, and threw it into contrast with its relighted surroundings. The original 1958 lighting equipment could not readily be replaced, and the subtle color scheme had been changed over time by inaccurate replacement parts. "The fountain lighting equipment and controls were outdated and needed to be replaced," says Michael J. McCambridge, senior vice president, Rockefeller Center Management Corporation.

FULFILLMENT

The fountain is surrounded by the umbrella-topped tables of the Summer Garden Restaurant at the American Festival Cafe. Passersby on the street level above have a birds-eye view as well.

For the fountain's relighting, Abe Feder created a more complex, synchronized, 26-minute long, multi-colored light and water spectacle. Feder's new lighting allows Prometheus to dominate. "The lighting and water are backdrop and trimming for the sculpture," Feder says. "The fixtures are positioned so the colors cast seem to generate from within the statue, and avoid a flat feeling of being 'stuck on'."

The only real limitation in designing the new scheme was the size of the space. Front to back the fountain measures 16.75 feet. The pool is 34 feet wide. Feder used 139 fixtures submersed into the pool and around the inside perimeter, integrated with a multitude of water jets.

The water configuration that existed for the first lighting has been retained. Feder added a curtain of water that rises up in front of the sculpture. New nozzles and variable speed pumps also have been installed.

The new 1,000-watt PAR 64 lamps used for the lighting are housed in the fountain's existing gasketed castings, made of bronze to resist pitting and deterioration from water. The fixtures are fitted with split glass filters in varied colors. The splits relieve pressure and guard against breakage from the pounding of the water, and the glass's expansion caused by heat from the lamps.

A computerized, electronic control board has been installed to handle the approximately 140 light and water cues needed for the 26-minute sequence. The program is stored on hard copy computer discs so the next generation will have it as well.

Towards the end of the 26-minute show sequence, the curtain of water rises up to conceal the sculpture as prelude to the finale, which highlights the crowning achievement of the mythical Greek figure—bringing fire to man. The water wall in front of the sculpture climbs and appears stormy grey and yellow. After changing quickly to a fiery red appearance, the water wall drops to reveal Prometheus holding the flame aloft and strikingly bathed in the same fiery glow.

The front water wall is pitched slightly towards the sculpture, so those seated in the outdoor restaurant adjacent to the fountain aren't splashed. The droplets of water splashed on the sculpture, however, make it sparkle and glisten, and contribute added dimension.

Setting up and programming the fixtures took about three weeks. The show runs continuously and automatically from dusk until about 1:00 A.M. daily, spring through fall.

Feder notes, when designing fountain lighting, it is important to know the limitations and characteristics of the light source selected, because at least 30 percent of the light transmitted is lost due to the water. Color filters decrease transmission and brilliance even more. A rich blue filter can cut about 80 percent light transmission, according to Feder. Bright pink allows only about 60 percent transmission.

Project: **Prometheus Fountain at Rockefeller Center**   Location: **New York, New York**   Client: Rockefeller Center Management Corporation
Lighting Designer: **Abe Feder, Lighting By Feder**   Project Team: **Michael J. McCambridge,** senior vice president; **William Stoddard;** and **Dennis Rehn,**
Rockefeller Center Management Corporation   Water Consultants: **Wet Industries Inc.**   Photographer: ©Elliott Kaufmann
Lighting Manufacturers: **General Electric Company**—*lamps;* **Sterner Lighting Co.**—*retrofit fixtures;* **Simes Co.**—*housings;* **Kliegl Bros.**—*Performer IV Digital Control Console*

Moments from the 26-minute long, computer controlled water and light show that plays out the legend of Prometheus, the Greek mythical teacher who brought fire to man.

TOKIO MONUMENT

158

CRITERIA

Kawagoe City, dubbed "Little Edo" (Edo is the ancient name for Tokyo), has origins which date back to the fifteenth century. The one-time castle town still has ancient houses lining the streets.

In early 1988, the city began to redevelop the area adjacent to the east exit of Japan Railway's Kawagoe Station. The landscape architects, Takeo Sato and Associates, realized that an air duct installed in the center of the station had the potential of becoming an important element in the new landscaping to be created in front of the station. And so, the designers, in conjunction with architect and lighting designer, Hisakazu Fujita, set about making this air duct a monument that would symbolize the growing vitality of the plaza and its surrounding district.

The goal for this project was to create a structure that embodied the essence of Little Edo. Fujita and the design team tied the Tokio monument they created at the air duct aurally and visually with the nearby Toki-no-kane, a historic bell that has been tolling for 350 years in the old town. At 16.64 meters tall by 8.35 meters wide, Tokio is nearly as large as the Toki-no-kane bell tower. The light and sound performances developed for the Tokio monument coincide with the bell's tolling.

FULFILLMENT

Tokio, the monument of Little Edo, is a polyhedron composed of several tetrahedrons—a composite of multiple, angled triangular faces on each side. Set into its iron frame are stainless steel, polished stainless steel (mirrored) panels, engraved aluminum panels, and black aluminum. The Tokio is animated with a variety of incorporated lighting elements.

Natural light plays on the angled panels—by day, the movements of the sun and the clouds are reflected on the mirrored panels; by night, the moon and stars.

From late evening to almost midnight, the black aluminum base is lit by high-pressure sodium lamps concealed in the monument. The warm glow from this light source is in contrast to the cool lights glowing below the nearby pedestrian decks. "This quiet technique, combined with the black panels on the upper monument and the warmly illuminated plantings at the base, helps to make Tokio look as if it is firmly rooted in Mother Earth," says Fujita.

"The water pattern is a traditional Japanese triangular pattern, which originated in the scales of fish. It implies bright beauty, swarming creatures, and a charm against evil. We used it to capture the gaiety of Kawagoe City's downtown district, the Kawagoe Station where many people come and go, and the Kawagoe citizens' wish for further development of the city," says Fujita.

At sunset, water patterns are created on varied surfaces of the monument by neon that shines through the engraved aluminum panels. This indirect light from the concealed, shielded source is directed out by reflective panels inside the monument. The illumination is softly tinted with a warm color as a reminder to viewers of traditional Japanese wood prints.

At 6:00 P.M. and 9:00 P.M., the monument goes dark, except for the cool surface-mounted neon that outlines the faces of the polyhedron. Then for three minutes, a xenon searchlight mounted inside the top of the monument begins to "salute" the old Toki-no-kane bell, two kilometers north. Synthesized music, synchronized with the movement of the light, tells the time. Then the searchlight-projected beam moves in the sky between north and south.

At 10 minutes after the hour, every hour after 5:00 P.M. (and for five minutes before midnight), a Y-shaped Japanese hemp leaf pattern—which exists also as decoration in a large hall in the ancient Kawagoe Castle—is created by warm neon which radiates directly from inside the monument's engraved surfaces. In this case, the rear of the light sources is shielded from the reflecting panels inside the monument.

Tokio sings a melody for about 25 seconds at noon, 6:00 P.M., 8:00 P.M., 9:00 P.M. and 10:00 P.M.. The melody, composed by Taizo Imao, has a bass part that represents today and a range of higher tones that represent tomorrow.

At midnight, the xenon light is cast again from the top of the monument vertically into the dark sky, as though it were recording what happened today and announcing the beginning of tomorrow.

This project received a 1991 International Illumination Design Awards Paul Waterbury Award of Excellence from the Illuminating Engineering Society of North America.

The monument is a polyhedron composed of varied tetrahedrons.

Project: **Tokio Monument in Little Edo**   Location: **Kawagoe, Saitama, Japan**   Owner: **Kawagoe City Office**
Architect: **Hisakazu Fujita, ALS Landscape Design Associates**   Landscape Architect: **Takeo Sato and Associates, Toda Landscape Planning, Fukken Engineering**
Lighting Designer: **Hisakazu Fujita, ALS Landscape Associates**   Contractor: **Kajima, Nishimatsu, Hatsuga & Nisshin JV, Iwabori & Kawamoku JV,**
Yamagiwa Lighting System Corporation   Photographer: **Toshio Kaneko**   Lighting Manufacturers: **Yamagiwa Corporation**

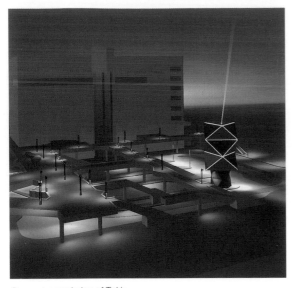

Computer rendering of Tokio.

Monument by day, which makes artistic use of an air duct.

A view at dusk shows Tokio in sync with its surrounding environment.

At night neon blue outlines are part of Tokio's animated light and sound show.

The surrounding electric lighting reflects on Tokio's metal panels.

The monument performs varied lighting shows at different hours throughout the day and night.

OSLO TOWER

CRITERIA

This tower, built in 1988 in Oslo's main railway station, was originally planned to be unilluminated. However, local residents disliked the tall, dark structure, and so to gain popular acceptance, the railway company decided to use light to improve the structure's appearance. The firm of Lighting Design Partnership, based in Edinburgh, Scotland, was retained to accomplish the task.

FULFILLMENT

The designers, Jonathan Speirs, IALD, Graham Phoenix, and Mark Major decided to capitalize on the propensity of Norwegians to enjoy free time, especially weekends. They named the structure the "Tower of Time," and devised a plan that would mark time throughout the week with progressively building illumination as Friday came closer.

A different lighted look was established for each day of the week, for winter and summer (warm in winter, cool in summer), for festival days and even for each year. A goal achieved by the scheme was minimizing the appearance of fixture hardware.

The rectangular form of the tower is delineated with white neon. The internal spiral staircase is lit with cool metal halide in summer, and high-pressure sodium in winter.

The tower lighting is fully automated. The progression of light builds vertically from Sunday to Friday via clear glass tubes filled with neon gas positioned in horizontal bands. On Sunday, for example, only white shows, and on Monday, the build-up of colored light segments begins. Chase sequences are programmed for Saturdays, Norwegian National Day, Christmas, and New Year's Day.

Fixtures at the top of the tower allow for a color change each year. The neon is automatically dimmed at dusk so it is not too strong for nighttime viewing. A neon analog clock and the client's logo are included on the panels on each side at the top of the tower.

This project received a 1991 Lighting Design Award Citation from the U.S.-based International Association of Lighting Designers. Jonathan Speirs is also the recipient of the Arets Belysning Diplom 1992, the first architectural lighting award bestowed by the Lyskultur organization, which claims to be the oldest cultural lighting organization in the world.

Project: **Oslo Tower**   Location: **Oslo, Norway**   Client: **Norwegian State Railways**   Architects: **HRTB (Ole Mowe), Oslo, Norway**
Lighting Designers: **Jonathan Speirs, IALD (now head of his own firm, Jonathan Speirs & Associates, with offices in Edinburgh and London), Graham Phoenix and Mark Major, Lighting Design Partnership**   Contractor: **Siemens**   Photographer: **Jo-Grim Gullvag**   Lighting Manufacturers: **Elektrovakuum, Siemens. Electrosonic supplied and adapted by Audio Grafisk, Oslo.**

The automated lighting marks the days of the week and special occasions.

LIGHTSCAPE '89

CRITERIA

The IBM building was transformed into a work of art by night for four nights in August 1989 by artist John David Mooney, who was invited to devise a special means of celebrating the 75th anniversary of the company in Chicago.

The IBM building is located in the middle of the city, bounded by Wabash, Kinzie, and State Streets, adjacent to the Chicago River, and tall enough to be visible from Lake Michigan. Mooney was fortunate to have as his "canvas" the sleek and striking regional headquarters building designed by architect Mies van der Rohe, founder of International Style school of architecture.

Van der Rohe used optical illusions to create a uniform appearance in the skyscraper. Mooney opted to design a light sculpture that would utilize the 7,192 windows of the building to create colorful and striking patterns that would contrast with its daytime image.

Mooney had only a couple of months to thoroughly plan what was to appear in each window and when, and to acquire, order, plan and organize how each task was to be accomplished. Increasing the challenge was this additional responsibility: Mooney was commissioned by the City of Chicago to design a searchlight ballet on the lakefront as part of the week-long celebration known as Chicago International Sky Nights. Called Light Dance '89 (photos included here), this event, which consisted of a light ballet achieved using World War II carbon arc searchlights, was scheduled to coincide with the final evening of Lightscape '89.

FULFILLMENT

Mooney worked on both projects simultaneously, writing a visual score for the movements of the lights, timed down to seconds. Meantime, a "Light Brigade" of one hundred volunteers was recruited to rehearse and perform the artwork. In addition to this Light Brigade, many more volunteers were recruited—for a total of over 200—to attend to all the details of equipment installation and coordination to bring the two artworks alive.

For Lightscape '89, each of the 5,500 incandescent custom-fabricated fixtures consisted of a socket bolted at an angle to a triangular base of aluminum and fitted with a 150-watt PAR floodlamp. The floodlamps were colored—red, blue, amber and white—and generously donated by Philips Lighting. An additional 192 rotating beacons in blue and white were donated by the Federal Signal Corporation.

But that's not all. One hundred-twenty aluminum, totem-like sculptures were fabricated at the artist's studio in Indiana to house tungsten-halogen automobile head lamps. Each sculpture had ten lamps and each lamp was covered with a blue Plexiglas lens. All of these lighting elements had to be powered by the building's 120-volt supply system.

The artist experimented with the visual impact created by varied light sources and techniques at the building by night before combining the incandescent lamps with kinetic rotating beacons, and tungsten-halogen totems, and opting to diffuse the effects by paper covering each window.

Mooney created more than 62 drawings, most measuring 5 feet high, to arrive at the design solution. Fifty-two architectural plans were drawn up for each of the floors, with each plan identifying the floor, every window, the type and color of lamp and where in each office it was to be placed, and the exact color of paper to be placed over individual windows. More than 11 miles of brown and white paper were cut to length for each of the 9-foot-high windows. Only one light source was used in each window.

After each evening's performance, at 2:00 A.M., it was necessary to restore the building for use by its daytime occupants.

Lightscape '89 received a 1991 Paul Waterbury Special Citation from the International Illumination Design Awards Program of the Illuminating Engineering Society of North America.

Project: **Lightscape '89 (and Light Dance '89)** © 1989, John David Mooney
Location: **Chicago, Illinois**   Client: **IBM**   Light Artist: **John David Mooney,**
John David Mooney Studio   Photographers: **Mooney, Barbara Jones,**
Les Boschke Photography   Lighting Manufacturers: **Philips Lighting,**
Federal Signal Corporation, General Motors

Mooney

The Lightscape '89 performance lasted from dusk until 2:00 A.M. on each of four nights.

Colored papers placed in each window were
used as diffusers in Lightscape '89.

Artist John David Mooney experimented with
mock-ups and computer graphics to produce
the giant light sculpture.

John David Mooney's "script" for Light Dance
'89 is much like a detailed orchestra's score.

Light Dance '89 involved a light ballet using
World War II carbon arc searchlights.

The fourth night of Lightscape '89 coincided with the lakefront searchlight ballet performance entitled Light Dance '89.

Kinetic and stationary lights in over 7,000 windows formed the basis of the Lightscape '89 light sculpture.

The shafts of light in Light Dance '89 pierced the blackness of the night sky and were set against the darkness of the adjacent lake.

LASER ART PERFORMANCES

CRITERIA

In Europe and Japan, outdoor laser and projection light and sound shows as expressions of cultural, commemorative and religious festivals and events have been increasing in popularity in recent years. Here is featured a collection of highlights of the laser shows created by lighting designer Motoko Ishii throughout Europe and Japan that use light as the paint on the canvas of a darkened universe.

FULFILLMENT

Laser Art Performance in Vienna

Carried out in the square in front of Vienna's Rathaus (City Hall), this laser art performance was one of several events in the 120th anniversary celebration of Austro-Japanese friendship held in October 1989, following the Europalia festival in Brussels. A multi-national team of professionals from Japan, Germany and Austria were assembled to create the performance, which drew approximately 8,000 participants.

Under clear skies, the crowd watched laser beams projecting patterns and giant images of Japanese scenery onto the building's wall, and a kinetic light performance in which colors changed from amber, to magenta and emerald. The lighting equipment was safely mounted on the rooftop and balcony of the building.

The three-part, two-hour program ended with the projection of the Japanese and Austrian national flags on the Rathaus wall.

Laser Performance in Brussels

Europalia is a cultural festival sponsored once every two years by Belgium. "Japan" was selected as the theme for the 1989 festival, in which varied aspects of Japanese culture were to be explored and celebrated. One of the events was a laser performance planned and produced by Motoko Ishii.

The 90-minute show was held in the Grand Place in the heart of Brussels, an ancient plaza surrounded by ornate structures built in the Middle Ages. About 12,000 spectators crowded into the plaza to view the evening performance, which was marked by giant changing patterns, images, and Japanese characters created with argon and krypton laser beams covering one wall of the City Hall, and the illumination of the entire building with colored lights.

Synthesizer music composed by Yoshitaka Azuma heightened the excitement of those who viewed the environmental art show.

Son et Lumiere in Miyajima

The Son et Lumiere is a light and sound show in which light is applied to historical structures and natural scenery, with a story told through sound and narration. The first Son et Lumiere was held at an ancient castle by the Loire River in France in the 1950s. In the summer of 1989, a Son et Lumiere show, with lighting designed by Motoko Ishii, was held in Japan at the Itsukushima Shrine, one of the satellite event areas of the Sea & Islands Exposition then being held in Hiroshima.

The huge Torii gate and shrine building, which is a national treasure, were softly illuminated to create an impression of moonlight. The stone lanterns lining the beach approach to the shrine were also illuminated, and giant images of Heikenoukyo and old Chinese ships were projected onto the sandy beach and rows of pine trees.

The audience enjoyed the performance, enhanced by the music and narration heard through earphones. Masatake Kitamoto was the producer of the show and Katsuhisa Hattori composed the music; Yoshiko Mita and Yoshio Kanauchi were narrators.

Laser Art Performance for the Shiga Sacred Garden

The Senzasai is a ceremony that involves moving the body of the God from Kyoto to the newly constructed House of God in the Shiga Sacred Garden, of Shinji Shumei-kai, a religious organization of the Shinto sect. To celebrate this significant religious occasion, a three-hour laser performance was carried out in an outdoor plaza and inside the sanctuary building at night.

The three-part ceremony included the pointing out of the directions of the moon and stars by laser beams, and the casting of the Shumei-kai's symbol in the clouds.

The main part of the performance held in the sanctuary included changing and colorful patterns of pure laser light, symbolizing the universe, time and man intertwined and suggesting the twenty-first century, coordinated with organ music. The epilogue was performed outdoors with spectators and the plaza wrapped in plays of split and reflected laser beams.

A 4-watt argon laser was used for the outdoor segments. A 4-watt argon and a 50-milliwatt helium neon laser were used indoors.

Projects & Locations: Son Et Lumiere, Hiroshima, Japan; Laser Art Performance, Brussels, Belgium; Laser Art Performance marking 120th anniversary of diplomatic relations between Japan & Austria Festival, Vienna, Austria; Laser Art Performance for Shiga Sacred Garden, Shiga, Japan (client: Shinji Shumei-kai)
Architects: Itoh Architects & Associates for Shiga Sacred Garden project; Europalia '89 Japan in Belgium for the performance in Brussels
Lighting Designer: Motoko Ishii, Motoko Ishii Lighting Design Inc.
Photographers: Performance in Brussels, Lucille Feremans, Foto Elu; Performance in Vienna, Baltazair Korab, Helikon-Photo Ges.m.b.H; Son et Lumiere in Miyajima, Yutaka Sakai and Yutaka Kohno; Performance for Shiga Sacred Garden, Motoko Ishii Lighting Design Inc.

Laser beam on the Rathaus in Vienna.

Laser art projections on City Hall in Brussels.

Playful laser patterns on City Hall in Brussels.

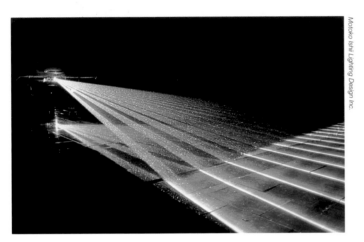

Merging laser patterns at the Shiga Sacred Garden.

Laser beam shining on raindrops at the Shiga Sacred Garden.

Laser patterns projected on clouds at the Shiga Sacred Garden.

The shrine illuminated at Son et Lumiere in Miyajirna.

The Torii gate lighted at Son et Lumiere in Miyajima.

Image of the Heian Period scroll paintings of Heikenoukyo project the sandy beach and trees at Son et Lumiere in Miyajima.

GIFU MEMORIAL CENTER,
WORLD LIGHTSCOPE

CRITERIA

Gifu Memorial Center, dubbed the king of sports arenas because of its 240,000 square meter area, is located at Nagaragawa Point in Japan. Built on the former site of the Gifu-Chubu Exposition, the center includes a variety of sports facilities, such as large and small domed gymnasiums, a track and field area, a baseball field, a martial arts building, tennis courts and other facilities.

World Lightscope, an integrated performance of light, sound and projected images, was part of the plan to entertain the city residents and visitors to this metropolitan park.

FULFILLMENT

The World Lightscope light and sound show included giant screens on which night scenes from around the world were projected so they could be seen and enjoyed from various viewing points. The light at each site changed to match the original music composed for this performance, creating the world's first integrated light environment performance system.

Special tri-colored (red, green and blue) filters were used in combination to create 120 different colors of light cast on the gymnasiums, track and field area, baseball field and other major sports areas. In addition, the world's largest laser system was installed above the track and field area near the main entrance. From here, red, green and blue beams were projected to dance in the night sky over Gifu Memorial Center. These systems were controlled by a main control computer and satellite computers, preprogrammed to run automatically.

To be more specific, the World Lightscope performances were conducted in varied zones designated around the six sports facilities of the Gifu Memorial Center. The approach to the Center, Sun Sun Deck (a pedestrian deck), was the main viewing point, with performances carried out in six satellite computer-controlled zones (A-F). Zone A was the "welcoming space," with the light and sound performance centering around the symbol monument. The performances in Zones B and C included projections of the nightscape of North and South America, and Oceania on two baseball field screens (12 x 20 meters). Zone D has an independent, 25-meter-high tri-colored screen on which the Asian nightscape was shown. And zones E and F showed the European nightscape floating above the track and field stadium.

Each zone contains a computer, two 4.5 kilowatt giant projectors, and sound equipment, including a compact disc player doing double duty as a program timer installed in a compact cylinder. With this equipment, music was used to enhance each country's light projection, and the light was changed freely to add visual life to the performance. The main computer and laser system, which controlled the entire performance were housed on the top floor of the track and field stadium.

Project: **Gifu Memorial Center, World Lightscope**   Location: **Gifu, Japan**   Client: **Gifu Prefecture**
Architect: **Nikken Sekkei Co., Ltd.**   Lighting Designer: **Motoko Ishii, Motoko Ishii Lighting Design Inc.**
Photographer: **Motoko Ishii Lighting Design Inc.**

The pedestrian deck served as the main viewing point for World Lightscope.

The welcome gate for World Lightscope.

Each zone contains a computer, two giant projectors and sound equipment.

Lighting is changed freely to add life to the performances.

AMERICAN'S SKY SCULPTURE

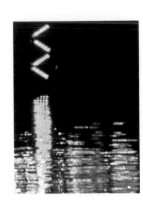

CRITERIA

American Airlines wanted to do something special to celebrate the dedication of their new terminal at Chicago's O'Hare International Airport, and so commissioned artist John David Mooney to create a unique work that, as a gift to the citizens of Chicago, would be performed in the center of the city.

Mooney chose to illuminate space and sky in Chicago for four days in May 1990 with a performance barge and programmed searchlight ballet. The resulting artwork, seen for miles, attracted thousands and involved the participation of hundreds of people.

FULFILLMENT

In addition to the artistic accomplishment embodied in the artwork, Mooney's achievement is found as well in the large-scale coordination and cooperation of people, materials, logistics and contingencies. The interrelationships formed among those who come together to assemble and perform the kinetic light sculptures in public places for the enjoyment of thousands are a trademark of much of Mooney's art.

The project involved almost 400 volunteers—American Airlines employees, architects from the Chicago area and the School of Architecture at Ball State University, and artists and engineers from Illinois and Indiana—who set up, rehearsed and performed the work.

For American's Sky Sculpture, Mooney designed a 65-foot-long by 35-foot-wide barge to float along the Chicago River in celebration of the evolution of transportation, from the waterways' role as a means of exploration, to the development of land-spanning railways, and sky-soaring airplanes. The barge was equipped with two, 220-watt argon lasers with fiberoptics, a 480-volt generator, two computers, and 1,000 tungsten-halogen lamps suspended from a Unistrut frame donated by Ball State University, and capped with 20, 20-foot-high red, blue and yellow lighted windsocks that rotated with the wind.

The barge was pulled to its site on the Chicago River east of Michigan Avenue, after an eight-hour journey, by Captain Egan's tugboat.

The barge's light show was set against a night sky filled with the beams of 36 carbon arc, World War II vintage searchlights placed on the north and south sides of the Chicago River east of Michigan Avenue, extending beyond Lake Shore Drive. Mooney composed a 900-page "score" for the four evenings—an evening of dress rehearsal, followed by three consecutive evening performances. Each evening included a precision light ballet with 97 distinct movements, many of them multi-phased within themselves.

The synchronization of the searchlights and barge lighting was directed via radio from the command center on the 42nd floor of the Swiss Grand Hotel.

The behind-the-scene arrangements included obtaining permissions from the landowners along the Chicago River, the Federal Aviation Administration, and varied city departments and agencies. The presentation was heightened with the cooperation of tenants and owners in surrounding buildings, who turned off the lights. All of the lights in The Wrigley Building, except in the tower, were turned off for the first time since World War II.

American's Sky Sculpture has been awarded a Chicago Illumination Design Award by the Chicago Section of the Illuminating Engineering Society of North America in recognition of outstanding achievement in lighting design.

Project: **American's Sky Sculpture** © 1990 John David Mooney
Location: **Chicago, Illinois**   Client: **American Airlines**   Light Artist: **John David Mooney, John David Mooney Studio**   Photographers: **Mooney, Barbara Jones**
Lighting Manufacturers: **Fisher Guide/General Motors, Philips Lighting**

Varied views of American's Sky Sculpture, which consisted of a performance barge equipped with lasers and fiberoptics juxtaposed against a night sky filled with projected moving beams from 36 World War II carbon arc searchlights.

Mooney

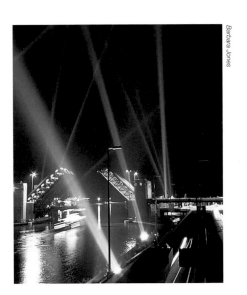

Barbara Jones

Barbara Jones

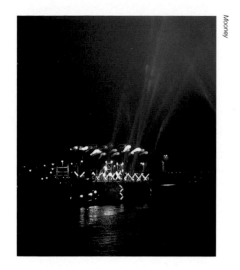

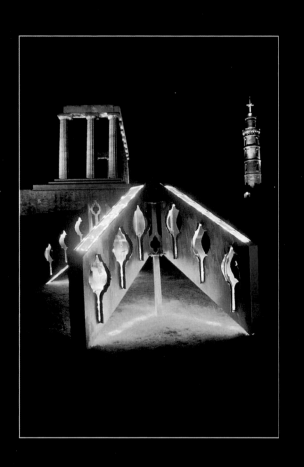

CHAPTER 6

LIGHT AS ART

Light can affect one's moods, reactions and perceptions. It can be exciting, fun and enlivening. This chapter celebrates the magic of light, and the ability to enjoy it as captured in outdoor works of art.

Light as an enhancer and clarifier is seen in the thoughtful illumination of the *Pledge of Allegiance* sculpture at Talon Centre, and the *Sun Ribbon* glass art wall, heightening the appreciation of these artworks by night. Light as an artwork itself is represented here by *The Grail*, in which colored light is not only visually pleasing, but reflects the deeper spiritual meanings behind the piece.

Light is interplayed with metallic surfaces to produce a transformed nighttime image for the sculpture, *Utsurohi*. And a multi-media, politically based art event, *enLight*, is detailed, which includes a kinetic searchlight ballet, whimsical grazing "electric sheep," and a *Holyrod Sculpture*.

PLAZA TOWER

CRITERIA

There are two parts to the Plaza Tower project. First, lighting designer Tom Ruzika, The Ruzika Company, was assigned the task of creating lighting for the 475,000 square foot Plaza Tower, the only stainless steel building in Orange County, designed by Cesar Pelli in association with CRSS Architects.

The owner of the Plaza Tower was also interested in including in the development an outdoor sculpture, *Utsurohi— A Moment in Movement,* created by the Japanese artist Aiko Miyawaki. "I was a consultant for the building lighting, and when the owner decided to commission the artwork, he asked me to make certain it was well lit," says Ruzika.

FULFILLMENT

The Plaza Tower is distinguished by two wide bands of light at the top made by two rows of 175-watt metal halide fixtures set on small ledges beneath the rows of windows. The long, narrow beam pattern creates an even glow of light on the "eyebrows." The maintenance of the lighting system is accounted for via one window that opens onto a ledge equipped with a safety cable used by the window washers as well as the lighting maintenance crew.

The workers on the two floors where the lighting is installed are protected from fixture glare. "The viewer looking out the window is aware that there is a light source outside, but the fixtures are positioned on just the right angle to prevent glare in the office occupants' eyes. Also, the bottom half of the window glass is tinted so darkly it acts as a glare shield," Ruzika explains.

The *Utsurohi—A Moment in Movement* sculpture is located on a grass-covered rectangle of land adjacent to the 21-story Plaza Tower office building. The sculpture was commissioned specifically because it incorporates the same element—stainless steel—that makes the Plaza Tower unique in Orange County.

The sculpture consists of 12 10-foot circular columns placed in an elliptical configuration and anchored to underground footings beneath the grassy ground cover. Each of the columns, covered with neoparies, a tile-like material, bears an engraved intaglio of one of the 12 animals of the Chinese Zodiac.

Each column is capped with a stainless steel baseplate on top of which is a stainless steel canister that houses the lighting. Twenty stainless steel, chromium-plated "threads" attached to the baseplates and extending out of the tops of the columns create graceful, flexible archways that connect one column to the next, and sway gently in the wind.

According to Miyawaki, "Utsurohi" refers to change—in seasons, the passing of the day, an hour or a second, the colors of the leaves, the sounds of a flowing stream, the successions of moods, the intertwining of dream with reality. It was appropriate, then, that Ruzika's lighting scheme for the sculpture embody movement and change as well.

Halogen PAR lamp fixtures are mounted flush with the ground in front and in back of each column. The units are also built into the top of each column, positioned very close to the rods. A preprogrammed dimming/control system carries out a series of crossfades over a 3 to 4 minute period, brightening and dimming the units in the caps, and in front and back of the columns until the cycle is complete.

Of course, Ruzika consulted extensively with Miyawaki during the lighting design process for the sculpture, and when it was completed, Miyawaki's response to Ruzika was, "You are breathing life into my art."

The computer controls are located in the parking garage a couple of hundred feet away. Ruzika explains that customers going to and from nearby restaurants are amazed by the sculpture, and sometimes stand in the center of it during the changing light show.

The Plaza Tower, located adjacent to the Orange County Performing Arts Center, is part of the South Coast Plaza area, which is filled with sculptures by artists such as Isamu Noguchi, Joan Miro, Henry Moore, and Carl Milles. And now, Aiko Miyawaki's artistry can be appreciated not only in the daytime, but during the night as well.

Project: **Plaza Tower & Utsurohi**　Location: **Costa Mesa, California**　Owner: **C.J. Segerstrom & Sons**　Sculpture Artist: **Aiko Miyawaki**　Architect: **Cesar Pelli, in association with CRSS Architects**　Landscape Architect: **Peter Walker & Associates**　Lighting Designer: **Tom Ruzika, The Ruzika Company**　Contractor: **Peck-Jones**　Photographer: **©1992 Jack Boyd**　Lighting Manufacturers: **Hydrel, Sterner Lighting**

The stripes of light at the top of the Plaza Tower building come from 175-watt metal halide fixtures set on ledges below the windows.

The Utsurohi sculpture is illuminated with halogen PAR fixtures ground-mounted in front of, behind, and in the tops of the columns.

SUN RIBBON SCULPTURE

CRITERIA

Problems with strong winds prompted a restaurateur in Costa Mesa, California, to commission artist Claire Falkenstein to create a stained glass work of art that would serve as a wind screen, rather than constructing a solid and ordinary partition. Creating a pleasing nighttime image for the wall of glass fell to lighting designer Tom Ruzika, The Ruzika Company.

FULFILLMENT

The work of art consists of multi-colored and textured pieces of glass that form a wall into which is integrated tall stone archways. "Stained glass can't be lit directly, and is meant to be looked through, so we needed to place light behind and around the wall to pull the eye through it," Ruzika says.

Ground-mounted halogen fixtures strategically placed near the bases of the archways uplight the archways and cast some spill light on the colored glass. The same fixtures have also been positioned near the building structure behind the glass wall so that the light "pulls the eye through," and creates irregular and intriguing patterns in the glass.

Project: **Sun Ribbon Sculpture**   Location: **Costa Mesa, California**
Owner: **C.J. Segerstrom & Sons**   Sculpture Artist: **Claire Falkenstein**
Lighting Designer: **Tom Ruzika, The Ruzika Company**
Photographer: **©1992 Jack Boyd**   Lighting Manufacturer: **Hydrel**

Because glass can't be lit directly, fixtures have been placed behind and around the stained glass wall.

TALON CENTRE

CRITERIA

The riverside building, which was constructed in the early part of this century to house Stroh's Brewery headquarters, was bought by the Talon Corporation, a holding company, and due for refurbishing. As part of the property's face-lift, the Talon Corporation opted to grace the building's circular driveway with a bronze sculpture, the *Pledge of Allegiance*, by artist George Lundeen.

It was the task of Gary Steffy Lighting Design Inc., working with photographs of the piece from the artist's studio, to design illumination to enhance the dusk and evening appearance of the sculpture year-round.

FULFILLMENT

Five ground-mounted fixtures fitted with 100-watt clear, 3200 degree Kelvin metal halide lamps provide general illumination that uplights the sculpture with a soft glow. Two spotlights, also using 100-watt clear metal halide lamps, focus on the flag.

Because the built-in reflector and refractor of the sophisticated fixture design allows for a 10-degree tilt, the possibility of the spotlight being misaligned accidentally by a maintenance crew is eliminated. "If you do your calculations correctly, you can locate the fixtures about three feet away from the flag and automatically have a spotlight falling on the flag, without having to adjust and aim the fixture," Steffy says. Since the fixtures also are flush with the ground, there are no protrusions to obstruct the view of the sculpture and surrounding plantings, or to be damaged by a passing lawn mower.

The addition of several pole-mounted fixtures surrounding the building was also a part of the renovation. "The Stroh's staff had redeveloped part of this site about 10 years ago," Steffy explains, "and there was a pole fixture that Howard Brandston had designed for them that they incorporated, had extras of and were willing to sell to Talon." The poles have been bought, but instead of being installed with the originally used mercury vapor light sources, a newer light source—the 3200 degree Kelvin metal halide lamp—has been added.

Teamwork is essential, regardless of the size of a project. And the fine cooperation shown by the landscape architect, Michael J. Dul Associates contributed to the success of this project. "He was very accommodating and helpful in the process of placing the fixtures, making sure plantings weren't obstructing the light throw or positioned in the location where the lights had to be placed," says Steffy.

The Talon Centre Corporation originally housed Stroh's Brewery headquarters.

The lighting is effective because it enhances the dramatic effect of the sculpture instead of calling attention to itself.

Project: **Talon Centre**   Location: **Detroit, Michigan**   Artist: **George Lundeen**   Landscape Architect: **Michael J. Dul Associates**
Lighting Designer: **Gary Steffy Lighting Design Inc.**   Contractor: **United Electric Co.**   Photographer: **©1993 Robert Eovaldi**   Lighting Manufacturers: **Hydrel, Winona**

ENLIGHT

CRITERIA

To commemorate and celebrate the European Summit, attended by all 12 heads of state in the European Community and held in Edinburgh, Scotland, in the winter of 1992, artist John David Mooney was commissioned to create a temporary, outdoor, multi-phase light sculpture/event. The site-specific piece would be an artistic expression of the manifestation of the "new Europe," symbolized by the summit. (Though Mooney is an American, he was invited as a European artist, because of his honorary Irish citizenship.)

FULFILLMENT

Mooney drew the iconography for the artwork from the chosen site in Edinburgh: the relationships of the area buildings—Edinburgh Castle, the Palace of Holyrod, Gosford House, and an eleventh-century abbey—to each other, and their interesting architecture and rich histories.

Situated on the second tallest hill in Edinburgh was the "Electric Sheep" sculpture, which consisted of 12 whimsical, grazing "sheep" constructed of wood and strings of low-voltage lights. Power was supplied by portable generators transported to the grassy knoll by the Scottish army. The sheep were visible to and enjoyed by the 12 heads of state, who resided at the Palace of Holyrod during the summit.

The second sculpture, called the "Holyrod Sculpture," was made of wood clad with shining aluminum, and adorned with built-in low-voltage lights. The yellow beacons, also included, symbolized flames. Emanating from the sculpture was a clear, bright projection of an ornate window frame pattern cast onto the facade of Gosford House. The frame was drawn from the architecture of an eleventh-century abbey, which stands adjacent to the Palace of Holyrod.

Mooney also created an earth drawing in the area by plowing patterns through 40 acres of fields. Inside the drawing, real live sheep grazed and roamed wearing genuine day-glo necklaces. This was accompanied by a nighttime show of light from strobe lamps—in blue and white, the colors of the Scottish flag—positioned on 30 telephone poles.

A searchlight ballet that illuminated the sky one evening from 9:00 P.M. to midnight, completed the artwork. Two squadrons of the Scottish army—one from Glasgow and the other from Edinburgh, were trained by a team of five architects and artists from the United States on how to move the searchlights to the "score" Mooney composed for the performance. The positioning and movement of each lamp for each moment of time was plotted and planned, very much like a musical score for an orchestra. The searchlights projected beams which danced about 8 miles up into the darkened sky.

Officials in London also wanted a sculpture created by Mooney to reflect what was taking place at the summit in Edinburgh. So in an indoor space overlooking the River Thames, Mooney created "enLight on Thames." In the first of two rooms, one glass wall allowed visitors an east to west view of the river. The changing daylight throughout the day cast light into the room which shone varied colors from rose through cool blue. Mooney installed blue lamps which created a futuristic triangular shadow rotating on one wall. On another wall, three projections on the aluminum frames of lamps cast light on the ground plane which was in turn reflected on the wall, like the play of light on the river rushing by just a few feet away.

The next room contained a wood sculpture with 180 rotating beacons attached to the projecting armatures. The effect on the viewer was hypnotic, as the beacons moved ever-changing bursts of light about the floor, walls and ceiling of the room.

Project: enLight (enLight on Thames) © 1992, John David Mooney
Location: Edinburgh, Scotland   Light Artist: John David Mooney, John David
Mooney Studio   Photographers: Mooney, Barbara Jones, Sam Dalkilic
Lighting Manufacturers: General Motors, Noma Lighting International,
Scottish Army—searchlights, Federal Signal Corporation

Electric sheep

Electric sheep

Electric sheep

Holyrod sculpture

enLight on Thames

Holyrod sculpture

Holyrod sculpture

Summit in the Sky

Summit in the Sky

Summit in the Sky

THE GRAIL

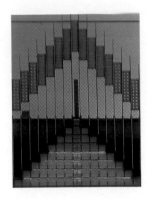

CRITERIA

Artist Lee Roy Champagne entered and won a contest sponsored by the San Francisco Arts Commission that encouraged submissions of artwork to adorn a building on Lombard Street in San Francisco. The building contains a first level leased to the U.S. Post Office and four levels of parking garages. The contest guidelines dictated that the sculpture fit on the flat facade approximately 13 feet wide and 40 feet tall that stands between the garage balconies which jut out on either side of it.

FULFILLMENT

Since the building was already existing, Champagne had to work with the architect, designers and engineers to integrate the sculpture completely through the foot-deep wall. Steel-encased service panels on the back side of the sculpture, accessible from inside the building, allow for maintenance and relamping of the system.

The sculpture goes beyond mere architectural graphics, and embodies a deeper significance as part of Champagne's body of artwork that includes light. "The sculpture is called 'The Grail'," says Champagne, "because my work deals primarily with a spiritual element. Light is a very spiritual force which is representational of healing, and hopes. Symbolically, it's been used as a metaphor for enlightenment and prosperity, and so this sculpture is an abstraction in a continuing series of pieces that speak of light as a spiritual energy force."

The sculpture is composed of neon, glass block, steel and aluminum. A vertical central shaft of clear glass block is flanked by four different patterns of block that create a cascade effect. The steel border around the glass block is painted a darker shade of the complexion of the building.

"All those colors represent different energy centers in the body, and are not just an abstraction of a rainbow effect," says Champagne. "The red at the base represents the mundane, earthly, physical plane. Then as one climbs up from that very narrow corridor, the spirit expands higher and higher to a greater evolution of consciousness." The sculpture culminates at the top with diamond-shaped glass block topped with a pyramid of aluminum rods and gridwork.

Although the sculpture was installed in 1988, it has been well maintained over the years, and looks the same today. The sculpture remains continuously illuminated, both day and night.

Champagne has worked with light since he was a child. "When I was young, I dealt with sculptures that incorporated incandescents and fluorescents. Then shortly before college, I started getting frustrated with the conventions of those mediums, and discovered neon. Neon was an evolution for me—I found out I could create any shape I wanted and that the spectrum is limitless." Today, Champagne has his own state-licensed vocational school, called the National Neon Institute, in Benecia, California, where, he says, "I teach people how to make neon." He also teaches neon art sculpture at the Academy of Art College in San Francisco.

Project: *The Grail* © Lee Roy Champagne
Location: **San Francisco, California**
Lighting Designer, Artist, Contractor: **Lee Roy Champagne**
Photographer: **Elan Santiago**

The Grail is composed of neon, glass block, aluminum and steel. The colors reflect the spiritual energy centers in the human body.

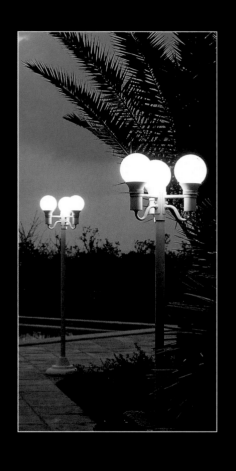

W PRODUCTS

Lighting product technology has advanced significantly in the past decade, resulting in the availability of a larger number of product types and sizes that allow lighting professionals greater freedom and creativity in their designs.

Refinements in light sources, for example, have led to smaller lamp packages, which in turn has led to the development of less bulky fixtures and housings. Now more than ever, landscape lighting can be accomplished with equipment so unobtrusive that the effects of light on the nighttime environment can be seen and appreciated, unencumbered by unsightly hardware.

At the same time, the reflector systems surrounding larger light sources and fixtures have been engineered to precisely produce incredibly long light throws useful in exterior building illumination. These heavy duty luminaires can lead to cost and energy savings in lighting designs, as a fewer number of fixtures is often needed to fulfill the lighting concept than in the past.

The past decade has seen a resurgence in the interest in neon, particularly in exterior retail applications. Color and

animation achieved with fiberoptics, searchlights, low-voltage incandescent lighting and other luminaire types have all become viable and commonplace options for bringing beauty and safety to the illuminated outdoor landscape. Pole-mounted fixture designs continue to run the gamut from historical to sleek contemporary, all with improved optics for precise beam control and elimination of unwanted spill, glare and light pollution.

Advancements in controls and dimming have not only extended lamp life in some cases, but enabled building owners cost and energy savings through the precise turn on and turn off of light fixtures.

Presented in the following pages of this chapter is a random sampling of products from many of the leading manufacturers of outdoor lighting. It is by no means complete, due to space limitations, as well as a puzzling lack of response from manufacturers who were invited to submit products for inclusion and opted not to by press time.

BEGA
P.O. Box 1285
Carpinteria, California 93014-1285
(805) 684-0533

The 8422 bollard is a straight-sided obelisk, 8 by 11/16 inches square with four "port" windows. The light distribution is even and efficient without glare. There is no closure glass in the windows. Instead, the lamp is enclosed and the light spread by a horizontal borosilicate glass lens. The unit features full illumination to the base of the fixture; a concealed lens, reflector, and lamp; vandal resistance; resistance to outdoor elements, such as dirt, water, and weather conditions; and solid, die-cast aluminum construction.

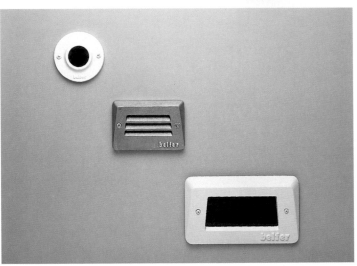

Belfer Lighting Manufacturing Co. Inc.
1703 Valley Road
Ocean, New Jersey 07712
(908) 493-2666

The Miniature Step Light series fills the three major requirements for step/aisle/platform lighting tasks: miniaturization, heavy-duty construction, and the ability to utilize an array of incandescent and fluorescent lamps. They are designed for interior and exterior applications. A variety of clear, frosted and treated Microlouver Photo-Osmetic film lenses are available to allow the specifier more flexibility.

Bronzelite
P.O. Box 606
San Marcos, Texas 78667
(512) 392-5821

The GM-6000 family of fixtures offers a choice of four different housing arrangements with optics ranging from compact fluorescent to 250-watt high-intensity discharge. The GM-6000 also features: composite housings, sealed optics, cam-latch closure system, Touch-Aim optics, encapsulated ballast, drive over construction, and a safety cutoff switch. The series is designed for specifier and contractor compatibility and engineered for fail-safe installation, operation and maintenance.

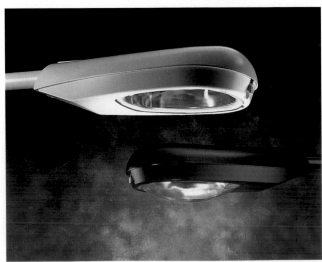

Crouse-Hinds
Division of Cooper Lighting
Highway 61 South
Vicksburg, Mississippi 39180
(601) 638-1522

This new series of high-intensity discharge luminaires, designed to provide outdoor lighting service on all types of roadways, are known as the OVY, OVF, and OVD. Available in Type 2 and 3 distribution patterns with cutoff ranging from medium to medium semi-cutoff, the new roadway lighting can be ordered in 48 different polyester powder coat finishes covering a wide spectrum of hues and shades. The OVY series uses a low-profile prismatic glass refractor, the OVF series uses a flat clear glass lens, and the OVD series has a traditional deep glass prismatic refractor.

Elliptipar, Inc.
114-152 Orange Avenue
West Haven, Connecticut 06516
(203) 931-4455

Elliptipar, Inc. has expanded its line of weatherproof outdoor fixtures with luminaires that accommodate tungsten
halogen lamps from 100 to 1,000 watts, high-intensity
discharge lamps from 70 to 800 watts, or fluorescent
lamps from 800 to 1,500 mA. These are designed to
place maximum light on the target surface with minimal
setback and profile. Each fixture begins with an asymmetric reflector designed to project light uniformly across
a surface from one edge that can orient light up, down,
or across surfaces. The fixtures allow for greater spac-
ing—at least 2 to 1, while being placed closer to the illuminated plane.

Fiberstars
47338 Fremont Boulevard
Fremont, California 94538
(510) 490-0719

Fiberstars 501 illuminator provides the state of the art in
fiber-optic lighting. It features a 400-watt, high-intensity
discharge lamp with a custom designed, solid-state
power supply for extraordinary brightness. Shown is an
application of Fiberstars fiberoptics in signage for
Holiday Inn. Also available is SuperStars fiber-optic tubing that emulates the look of a strip of tiny light bulbs, but
with no small bulbs to burn out.

GE Lighting
General Electric Company
Nela Park
Cleveland, Ohio 44112
(216) 266-2654

The 175-watt High Performance Halarc metal halide
lamp features improved efficiency, which is 22 percent
higher than other standard metal halide lamps. In addition, the High Performance Halarc offers longer life of
15,000 hours average rated life, which is a 50 percent
increase over standard metal halide lamps. The lamp
has good color with a color rendering index of 65 and a
color temperature of 3200 Kelvin. It operates on Electro-
Reg and MagReg ballasts and features a shorter hot
restart of less than four minutes.

GE Lighting
General Electric Company
Hendersonville, North Carolina 28739
(704) 693-2198

The Dimension Luminaires are a family of contemporary
square site lighting fixtures from mounting heights above
20 feet. Dimension fixtures can operate either high-
pressure sodium or metal halide sources in wattages
from 70 to 1,000 watts. The fixture is comprised of a
precision engineered aluminum housing featuring die
cast end caps and optical door for durability and light
weight. Finishes include standard dark bronze, white or
black. Pole top mounting options include both 4-inch
and 12-inch mounting arms, yoke-mounting, spider
mounting and an internal slipfitter to give users desired
flexibility.

Greenlee Lighting Inc.
A Subsidiary of LSI Industries Inc.
1510 Capital Parkway, Suite 110
Carrollton, Texas 75006
(214) 466-1133

The Garden Series from Greenlee includes fixtures in a variety of shapes, sizes, stem lengths and mounting arrangements. All fixture heads are cast aluminum. Each unit is finished with durable, powder-coat, polyester paint in a new interpretation of verde green. The reflective surfaces on the inside of each unit are painted white for enhanced performance. Incandescent lampholders are 4KV pulse rated, glazed porcelain with spring center contact. Fluorescent lampholders are high-temperature thermoplastic.

Hanover Lantern
Division of Hoffman Products, Inc.
470 High Street
Hanover, Pennsylvania 17331
(717) 632-6464

Shown is an installation of Hanover Lantern's Terralight Landscape Lighting Fixtures. Several versions of model 6300 are used to illuminate pathways; model 6313 provides spread lighting to light certain areas of ground cover, plants, and low shrubberies; and varied spotlights, including models 6377, 6378, LV119 and LV120 are used to highlight trees, plants, fencing and buildings.

Hanover Lantern
Division of Hoffman Products, Inc.
470 High Street
Hanover, Pennsylvania 17331
(717) 632-6464

The Augusta series 13400 includes a post-top lantern model, shown with black finish, clear bent beveled glass panels, solid brass finial, and solid brass three-light candelabra cluster. The dimensions are: 26 inches high, 10¼ inches wide, and it fits atop a 3-inch O.D. post. Five other models are also available in the series. Hanover Lantern decorative lighting fixtures, pole and accessories are constructed from commercial grade, heavy duty cast titanium/aluminum and non-ferrous fasteners to provide years of lasting beauty.

Holophane Company, Inc.
Unique Solutions Division
515 McKinley Avenue
Newark, Ohio 43055
(614) 349-4194

The Prismasphere models with internal refractor or external prisms provide up to twice the utilization of non-optical spheres while improving the uniformity of light and reducing glare. A variety of ballast housings are designed to match contemporary or historical style poles and posts. Spheres are available to accept 35- through 200-watt high-pressure sodium, metal halide, mercury vapor, or incandescent lamps. The version shown has three-way clear spheres with internal optics on a 10-foot round aluminum pole.

Holophane Company, Inc.
Unique Solutions Division
515 McKinley Avenue
Newark, Ohio 43055
(614) 349-4194

The GranVille prismatic glass acorn offers authentic historical styling with prismatic light control for maximum efficiency, uniformity and low brightness. Three heat-resistant borosilicate glass refractors are offered, designed for I.E.S. type III, IV and V lighting distributions. A variety of ballast housings are designed to match cast iron, aluminum, fiberglass or concrete posts. The luminaire is available with a hinged top, and can house a high-pressure sodium, metal halide, mercury vapor, low-pressure sodium or incandescent lamp from 35 to 250 watts. Shown is a GranVille with convex octagonal housing on a 10-foot Wadsworth cast aluminum post.

Hydrel
12882 Bradley Avenue
Sylmar, California 91342
(818) 362-9465

The 7000 Series Architectural Lighting System has four-way mounting orientation, from the ground, wall, ceiling or pole. Five basic light distributions are offered on the ground mount version. Optional internal glare control. The units are lamped to 175-watt high-intensity discharge. The tough, cast aluminum package is available with accessories. Hydrel offers a range of outdoor lighting products with advanced technology for sealing in-grade surface mount, wall mount, and underwater fixtures.

Hydrel
12882 Bradley Avenue
Sylmar, California 91342
(818) 362-9465

The 9400 Series Recessed Wall Lights, in round or square versions, are for high-intensity discharge sources to 100 watts, and incandescent sources to 150 watts. The fixtures feature a low-glare optical system and modular construction. Six beam distributions are available, and glare is significantly reduced without external louvers or special lenses. Installation is simplified with pre-installed back boxes and the addition of sealed components after construction. Size is reduced because of the open circulation. Trims and accessories are cast bronze or aluminum.

Kim Lighting
16555 East Gale Avenue
City of Industry, California 90803
(818) 968-5666

Tho Micro-Flood measures only 5½ inches wide by 6 inches tall, but offers the same aesthetic detailing and rugged construction of the company's larger AFL series of floodlights. Using quartz lamps up to 75 watts (120-volt or 12-volt) in conjunction with a sophisticated hydro-formed reflector, the Micro-Flood is able to perform floodlighting functions usually reserved for much bulkier fixtures. For narrower beam applications, 12-volt, MR 16 lamps can also be specified. Barn doors or fixed hoods are optional accessories.

King Luminaire Co., Inc.
P.O. Box 266
1153 State Route, #46
Jefferson, Ohio 44047
(416) 632-9301

The K118-E Washington Luminaire is a photometrically advanced fixture with the sparkling performance characteristics usually associated with more utilitarian lights. The unit with external refractor puts more light where you need it. Regarding the styling, of the many acorn globes that found their way onto the city streets of North America in the early 20th century, the 118 shape was perhaps the most widely used.

King Luminaire Co., Inc.
P.O. Box 266
1153 State Route, #46
Jefferson, Ohio 44047
(416) 632-9301

Probably the most versatile of all ornamental luminaires available in the first three or four decades of the 20th century, the K56 Octagonal Luminaire was originally used as a post top, a pendant and, on occasion, even a floodlight. It first appeared during the First World War, achieving instant approval as an acceptable alternate to the ever-popular acorns. The Octagonal today is offered in the Cleveland version (without spurs) and as the Tudor (with spurs). The optical system offers excellent photometric performance in IES Type III and V patterns with a wide variety of high-intensity discharge light sources. The rugged cast aluminum construction and modular ballast assembly of the K56 insure low cost and easy maintenance. A twistlock receptacle for a photocell is offered as an option.

LSI Industries Inc.
10,000 Alliance Road
Cincinnati, Ohio 45242
(513) 793-3200

The Seabrook Series includes a wide selection of mountings, housings, reflectors and detail options. The optional Glo-Top emits an upward glow; color Glo-Bands create a neon-line fluorescence effect to complement a building's accent color. The luminaires are available in 13 solid-colors and finishes. Accent decal stripes allow further color customization.

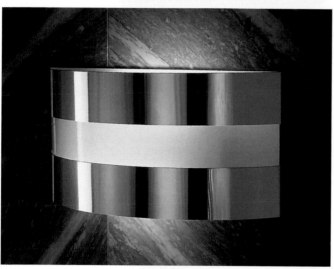

Lightway Industries
25345-213 Avenue Stanford
Valencia, California 91355

Lightway is offering a complete line of energy-efficient fixtures that meet ADA wall depth requirements, designed for interior and exterior use. The style of the St. Louis-4 is reminiscent of the St. Louis arch with its sweeping solid brass arches separated by a diffused band of light. Constructed of heavy gauge steel, finished in brass with chrome or powder coated colors and equipped with a white textured acrylic lens, the St. Louis is 14 inches wide, 4 inches deep and 7 inches high, and is UL listed for damp locations.

Lumark Lighting
Division of Cooper Lighting
Highway 61 South
Vicksburg, Mississippi 39180
(601) 638-1522

The Lumark Caretaker low-voltage, high-intensity discharge outdoor security fixture is designed to complement both commercial and residential environments in a ceiling or wall mount application. It is offered in white or architectural bronze, with a choice of 35-watt or 50-watt high-pressure sodium lamps. Compared to typical outdoor fixtures using two 150-watt PAR lamps, the Caretaker could save users about $93.00 per fixture per year (based on an energy charge of 0.7 cents per kilowatt hour).

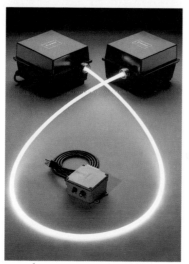

Lumenyte International Corporation
350 Lear Avenue
Costa Mesa, California 92626
(714) 556-6655

Lumenyte solid core, spliceable fiber-optic systems are available for use with both high-intensity discharge and quartz halogen light source. Units are offered with flexible or semi-rigid, heat shapeable fiberoptics. Applications include building accents, water features, steps, pathways, glassblock, displays, special effects, and light sculptures.

Lumiere Design & Manufacturing, Inc.
31360 Via Colinas #101
Westlake Village, California 91362
(818) 991-2211

The Sanibel #806 is designed to function as an accent, flood or general area illuminator. Using a 120-volt PAR 20 (50-watt maximum) lamp in a lensed and sealed housing, the 806 delivers a powerful punch from virtually any location. The fixture is machined from high-grade aluminum and finished with a chromate conversion coating and a baked thermoplastic polyester powder paint. It can accept hexcell louvers and color filters.

Noral Lighting, Inc.
P.O. Box 360532
Cleveland, Ohio 44136
(216) 273-7155

Noral Lighting offers a complete line of high-quality, cast-aluminum outdoor fixtures including exterior wall mounts, surface mounts, commercial-size, high-intensity discharge parking lot fixtures and posts, and a complete bollard package. A traditional family of fixtures is available in matte black, white and patina green finishes. The new compact line shown is offered in ten additional glossy colors and is ETL approved.

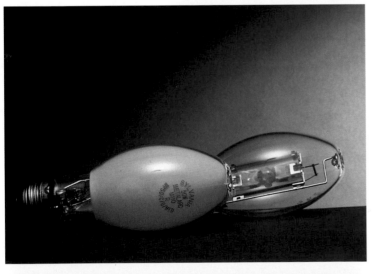

Osram Sylvania Inc.
100 Endicott Street
Danvers, Massachusetts 01923
(508) 777-1900

The 50-, 70-, and 100-watt Metalarc Pro-Tech lamps fit medium base sockets and can be used in open bottom fixtures. The lamps come with a clear or coated bulb. Initial lumens are 3300, 5500 and 8500 for clear lamps; 2800, 4800 and 8000 for coated lamps. The lamps can be burned in any position. The 50-watt lamp has an average rated life of 5000, while the 75- and 100-watt units are rated at 10,000 and 7500 hours for the vertical and horizontal positions, respectively.

Osram Sylvania Inc.
100 Endicott Street
Danvers, Massachusetts 01923
(508) 777-1900

The 60-watt Capsylite halogen lamp has a special reflector design that produces a powerful beam of light, allowing designers to use it in place of significantly higher wattage incandescent spots and floods. The Capsylite lamps are designed with a small halogen capsule inside the bulb. The filament inside the capsule operates at a higher temperature resulting in a whiter light source, at 3000 degrees Kelvin. Also the halogen cycle inside the capsule is such that there is no blackening of the glass, which means light output is retained over lamp life.

Poulsen Lighting, Inc.
5407 NW 163 Street
Miami, Florida 33014-6130
(305) 625-1009

The Columbus bulkhead fixture has been designed for use with both compact fluorescent and high-intensity discharge lamps. The unit has a triangular perforated metal controlling shield, giving a more directional downward illumination, yet at the same time offering ambient illumination up and outward. Columbus is made from durable materials that meet the unpredictability of both climatic elements and people.

Reggiani USA
65 River Road
P.O. Box 4270
New Windsor, New York 12553
(914) 565-8500

WetScape, designed by Carlo Vietri, is appropriate for both indoor and outdoor use. The fixture is constructed of die-cast aluminum with a continuous gasket and tempered clear glass lens. The units are designed to provide maximum heat dissipation through conduction and radiation to maximize lamp life. The swivel is fully adjustable, with 350-degree rotation and 112-degree angulation. The lamp housing incorporates a "cool grip" aiming surface for exact positioning of the light beam. WetScape fixtures are available in white, black, graphite and landscape green finishes and accommodate 50-watt, MR 16 lamps indoors.

Shakespeare Electronics and Fiberglass Division
P.O. Box 733
Newberry, South Carolina 29108
(803) 276-5504

The Presidential Series of poles range from 9.5 to 30 feet tall. All styles are available with fluted or smooth tapered shafts. There are four different base styles offered, and all poles come in split shroud base, one-piece solid base or in slip-over base versions. Shown is a Washington style base with a fluted, tapered shaft. This base is offered in 17-, 20- and 28-inch diameter models. Presidential poles are available in standard direct burial style, and shipped with the direct burial foundation permanently factory installed.

Staff Lighting Corp.
300 Route 9W
P.O. Box 1020
Highland, New York 12528
(914) 691-6262

The Gamma lantern, reminiscent of old gas lanterns, seamlessly blends the past with present. Gamma's graceful cap encloses a variety of louvering options, including the MTR refractor, a mirror or white louver and a borosilicate refractor or a spherically spun louver. Gamma is available in single pole top, cluster or wall mount. A range of lamp types are available.

Staff Lighting Corp.
300 Route 9W
P.O. Box 1020
Highland, New York 12528
(914) 691-6262

Series 200 Bollards are manufactured of cast and extruded aluminum, are easy to mount, and are highly vandal-resistant. They are offered in the traditional round shape, or more unique, fluted profile, and with a variety of shielding options, including white louver, cast louver, fresnel glass lens or double conical reflector. A variety of lamp types can be used.

Staff Lighting Corp.
300 Route 9W
P.O. Box 1020
Highland, New York 12528
(914) 691-6262

Saturn luminaires are built on a graceful, human scale and designed to fill the lighting needs of town and country alike. All Saturns are available as single-pole top, wall brackets or clusters, and with mirror or white louvers, MTR (Multiprisms for Total Refraction) refractors or borosilicate refractors. A broad range of lamp types can be used, with fluorescent, metal halide, mercury or high-pressure sodium options available. Each luminaire has uv-stabilized polycarbonate shielding and countersunk stainless steel screws for increased vandal-resistance, and is gasketed for weatherproofing, dust and insect control.

Sterner Lighting Systems, Inc.
351 Lewis Avenue West
Winsted, Minnesota 55395
(612) 485-2899

The Infranor 895, a high-powered precision floodlight using the Infranor Segmented Optical System for clean beam illumination of high-rise structures, is ideal when lighting uniformity is critical. And the 895 allows such precise control that virtually all light spill is eliminated and optimum illumination is possible with fewer fixtures, less wattage and significant energy savings. The 895, designed for 1,000-watt metal halide or high-pressure sodium lamps is capable of producing a 9- by 24-degree up to a 40- by 100-degree beam, and offers both horizontal and vertical lamp positioning.

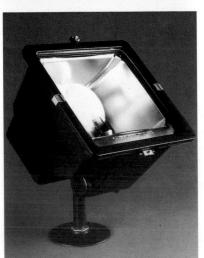

Thomas & Betts Corporation
1555 Lynnfield Road
Memphis, Tennessee 38119

The American Electric Lighting White Nite metal halide and Microwatt high-pressure sodium floodlights are available with the following standard features: die-cast aluminum housing; dark bronze baked-on enamel finish; normal- or high-power-factor ballasts; high-efficiency aluminum reflectors with narrow or wide beamspreads; impact and thermal shock resistant, tempered glass lens; factory pre-wiring; and adjustable yokes or locking knuckles with ½-inch threaded mounting arm for precise aiming. White Nite is offered in 50-150 watts; Microwatts in 35-150 watts.

Venture Lighting International, Inc.
32000 Aurora Road
Solon, Ohio 44139
(216) 248-3510

The MH 1500/U/XL is a long-life 1,500-watt metal halide lamp to be used in professional sports lighting and large area flood applications. The longer life is accomplished through the use of a revolutionary arc tube design. Venture Lighting also offers Low-Wattage, Open Fixture, Energy Master, White-Lux and PAR metal halide lamp families, as well as other lamp lines.

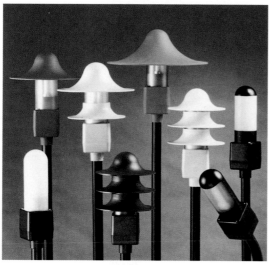

W. F. Harris Lighting
P.O. Box 5023
Monroe, North Carolina 28111-5023
(704) 283-7477

The Scapeform fluorescent landscape lighting fixtures have a ballast housing molded of tough, ultraviolet stable Makrolon 9417 polycarbonate resin. The lenses and shades for the fixtures are molded of Makrolon 2507 polycarbonate resin. (Both resins are from the Polymers Division of Miles Inc., Pittsburgh.) The Scapeform lighting fixtures are available in seven colors. Small, medium and large width shades can be mixed to fit the needs of the application.

Xenotech, Inc.
8211 Lankershim Boulevard
North Hollywood, California 91605
(818) 767-0365

The Automated Britelight 7000 is a five-function automated spotlight. These functions are tilt, pan, beam focus, color scrolling and a dowser. The color scroller can have up to 16 frames of color, including clear. The Automated Britelight 7000 operates on a standard DMX-512 protocol. It weighs 675 pounds in its case, and 450 pounds without the case or 185-pound external power supply.

APPENDIX 1
Lighting Awards

Illuminating Engineering Society of North America

The Illuminating Engineering Society of North America (IESNA) is the recognized authority in illumination. For over 85 years, its mission has been to promote good lighting practice and provide information to the lighting community for the benefit of society.

Some of the projects featured in this book have received awards in the IESNA's International Illumination Design Awards (IIDA) Program. The IIDA Program includes the Edwin F. Guth Memorial Awards, the Paul Waterbury Outdoor Lighting Awards, and the Aileen Page Cutler Memorial Award for Residential Lighting Design.

The IIDA Program serves the lighting industry by recognizing and honoring those who create pace-setting lighting design, providing lighting education by example. The program provides the opportunity for public recognition of professionalism, ingenuity, and originality in lighting design. Projects are judged individually on their own merits and not against each other. IIDA is open to all professionals in the lighting community, without limitations as to professional affiliations.

The awards program is administered by the IESNA through its IIDA Committee, with the help of region and section IIDA officers. Projects receiving consideration at the national IIDA judging have already been through two levels of judging at the IESNA section and region levels. Those advancing through the regional judging earn the Award of Merit and consideration for the national awards: Special Citation, Award of Excellence, and Award of Distinction.

The Edwin F. Guth Memorial Award is named after Edwin Guth, founder of the St. Louis Brass Co., later renamed Guth Electric. They are funded by a charitable trust established in 1965 by the Edwin F. Guth Co. The Guth Award was first presented in 1972.

The Paul Waterbury Award for outdoor lighting is named after the designer of the 1,500-watt metal halide lamp. The Waterbury Award was first presented at the 1989 IESNA Annual Conference and is sponsored by JJI.

The Aileen Page Cutler Memorial Award for Residential Lighting Design is donated by Monte Cutler and named after his late wife. It was established in 1991.

For more information about IESNA or its awards program, contact:
Illuminating Engineering Society of North America
120 Wall Street, 17th Floor
New York, New York 10005-4001
Tel. (212) 248-5000

International Association of Lighting Designers

The International Association of Lighting Designers (IALD), founded in 1969, has approximately 450 members worldwide. Voting membership is achieved through submission of a portfolio and review by the Board of Directors. IALD members are independent, professional designers, educators, or students of architectural lighting.

Each year the IALD recongizes lighting that displays high aesthetic achievement backed by technical expertise, and that exemplifies a synthesis of the architectural and lighting design processes via its Lighting Awards Program. As an ongoing collection of work, the awarded projects represent varied approaches to outstanding lighting design.

Two categories of awards are given: Awards of Excellence and Citations. Projects are judged individually, based on aesthetic achievement, technical merit and according to the designer's concepts and goals. It is not a competition.

Anyone may submit a project. The project must be a permanent architectural lighting design solution, interior or exterior, for which construction was completed by a specified deadline. Lighting products, equipment and design for theatrical performances are not eligible.

For more information on the Lighting Award or the IALD, contact:
International Association of Lighting Designers
18 East 16th Street, Suite 208
New York, New York 10003-3193
Tel. (212) 206-1281

APPENDIX 2
Directory

Architects and Lighting Designers

ALS Landscape Design Specialists
Livina 1-5-10 Sotokanda
Chiyoda-ku Tokyo, Japan 101
03-3253-2111

Baxter, Hodell, Donnelly & Preston
3500 Redbank Road
Cincinnati, OH 45227

C.M. Kling & Associates/Architectural
Lighting Designers
919 King Street
Alexandria, VA 22314
(703) 684-6270

C.W. Kim, AIA, Architectural Planners, Inc.
425 West B Street, Suite 202
San Diego, CA 92101
(619) 234-0555

Cannon
330 East 59th Street, Fourth Floor
New York, NY 10022-1537
(212) 486-6700

Craig A. Roeder Associates, Inc.
3829 North Hall Street
Dallas, TX 75219
(214) 528-2300

Dan P. Kopple & Associates
1611 Walnut Street
Philadelphia, PA 19103
(215) 568-7350

Gary Steffy Lighting Design Inc.
315 East Eisenhower Parkway, Suite 216
Ann Arbor, MI 48104
(313) 747-6630

Garner Perdue Associates
2105 Garnet Avenue, Suite C
Pacific Beach, CA 92109
(619) 270-0222

Goody, Clancy & Associates
334 Boylston Street
Boston, MA 02116
(617) 262-2760

HKS Architects
1111 Plaza of the Americas, 11th Floor
Dallas, TX 75201
(214) 969-5599

Halvorson Company, Inc., The
161 Massachusetts Avenue
Boston, MA 02116
(617) 537-0380

Hellmuth, Obata & Kassabaum, Inc.
1831 Chestnut Street
St. Louis, MO 63103
(314) 421-2000

Illuminart
404 North River Street
Ypsilanti, MI 48198
(313) 482-6066

John H. Anderson & Associates
1102 Oakfield Court
Roseville, CA 95661
(916) 773-2536

John David Mooney Studio
114 West Kinzie Street
Chicago, IL 60610
(312) 822-0483

Jonathan Speirs & Associates
34 Blair Street
Edinburgh EH1 1QR Scotland
031-226-4474

John Grissim Associates
400 Galeria Office Centre, Suite 555
Southfield, MI 48331
(313) 553-2500

Johnson, Johnson & Roy/inc
110 Miller Street
Ann Arbor, MI 48104
(313) 662-4457

Kling-Lindquist Partnership
2301 Chestnut Street
Philadelphia, PA
(215) 569-2900

Loebl Schlossman and Hackl, Inc.
130 East Randolph Drive, Suite 3400
Chicago, IL 60601
(312) 565-1800

Lighting by Feder
1600 Broadway, Suite 703
New York, NY 10019
(212) 262-0680

Mackey Mitchell Associates
800 St. Louis Union Station
St. Louis, MO 63103
(314) 421-1815

Michael J. Dul Associates
212 Daines Street
Birmingham, MI 48009
(313) 644-3410

Motoko Ishii Lighting Design Inc.
MIL Design House, 5-4-11 Sendagaya
Shibuya-ku, Tokyo, Japan 151
03-3353-5311

National Neon Institute
1070 Tyler Street
Benicia, CA 94510
(707) 747-6167

Neuman Smith & Associates
400 Galeria Office Centre, Suite 555
Southfield, MI 48034
(313) 352-8310

Peter Kaczorowski
63 Perry Street, #9
New York, NY 10014
(212) 807-8315

Quinn Evans Architects
119½ North Main Street
Ann Arbor, MI 48104
(313) 663-5888

Randy Burkett Lighting Design, Inc.
127 Kenrick Plaza, Suite 207
St. Louis, MO 63119
(314) 961-6650

Robert Singer & Associates
175 Fifth Avenue, Suite 2356
New York, NY 10010
(212) 369-1300

Ross De Alessi Lighting Design
4370 Alpine Road
Portola Valley, CA 94028
(415) 851-7950

Ruzika Company, The
16762 Mac Arthur Blvd., #319
Irvine, CA 92715
(714) 752-5003

SWA Group, The
401 Fairway Drive
Deerfield Beach, FL 33441
(305) 427-0666

Space Design International
4003 Pulido Court
Calabasas, CA 91302
(818) 222-4999

Space Design International
311 Elm Street
Cincinnati, OH 45202
(513) 241-3000

Space Design International
860 Broadway
New York, NY 10003
(212) 254-1229

Sterner Lighting Systems, Inc.
351 Lewis Avenue West
Winsted, MN 55395
(612) 473-1251

Steven M. Elbert, AIA
2491 Sherwood Road
Columbus, OH 43209
(614) 237-5977

Sylvan R. Shemitz Associates, Inc.
145 Orange Avenue
West Haven, CT 06516
(203) 934-3441

WGFS Lighting
5855 Green Valley Circle, #304
Culver City, CA 90230
(310) 216-1670

Wah Yee Associates
34405 West 12 Mile Road, Suite 225
Farmington Hills, MI 48018
(313) 489-9160

Wedemeyer Cernile Carrubia, Inc.
314 North Broadway, Suite 858
St. Louis, MO 63102
(314) 231-9377

Wheel Gersztoff Friedman Associates
5855 Green Valley Circle, Suite 304
Culver City, CA 90230
(310) 216-1670

William J. Johnson Associates Inc.
444 South Main Street
Ann Arbor, MI 48104
(313) 668-7416

Photographers

Alexander, Rick
Rick Alexander & Associates, Inc.
212 South Graham Street
Charlotte, NC 28202
(704) 332-1254

Bielenberg, Paul
6823 Pacific View Drive
Los Angeles, CA 90068
(213) 874-9951

Boschke, Les
Les Boschke Photography
1839 West Fulton
Chicago, IL 60612
(312) 666-8819

Boyd, Jack
2038 Calvert Avenue
Costa Mesa, CA 92626
(714) 556-8332

Broderick, Janice K.
A.G. Edwards Corporate Communications
One North Jefferson Avenue
St. Louis, MO 63117
(314) 772-4492

Bronzelite
500 Wonder World Drive
P.O. Box 606
San Marcos, TX 78667-0606
(512) 392-5821

Cable, Wayne
Cable Studios, Inc.
401 W. Superior
Chicago, IL 60610
(312) 951-1799

Cook, Robert Ames
135 Ganfield Place, #327
Cincinatti, OH 45202
(513) 241-1313

Cott, George
Chroma Inc.
2802 Azeele Street
Tampa, FL 33609
(813) 873-1374

D'Addio, James
12 East 22nd Street, #PH-4
New York, NY 10010
(212) 533-0668

Dalkilic, Sam
The Backwoods Gallery
P.O. Box 591
Cedar Lake, IN 46303
(219) 663-9371

Eovaldi, Robert
7834 Huron
Taylor, MI 48180
(313) 386-8314

Fentress, Sam
1047 South Big Ben Blvd.
St. Louis, MO 63117
(314) 645-7800

Feremans, Lucille
Foto Elu
Akkerstraat 75-77
9140 Temse, Belgium
03-771-06-95

Golden, Fred
1510 Franklin Avenue
Ann Arbor, MI 48104
(313) 663-2040

Golding, Robert
B & H Photographics
2045 Richmond Street
Philadelphia, PA 19125
(215) 423-0363

Gullvag, Jo-Grim
Jonathan Speirs and Associates
34 Blair Street
Edinburgh EH1 1QR Scotland
44-31-226-4474

HOK Photography
1831 Chestnut Street
St. Louis, MI 63103
(314) 421-2000

Hursley, Greg
4003 Cloudy Ridge
Austin, TX 78734
(512) 266-1391

Jones, Barbara
John David Mooney Studio
114 West Kinzie Street
Chicago, IL 60610
(312) 822-0483

Kaneko, Toshio
2-14 Minamiyamabushi-cho
Shinjuku-Ku Tokyo, Japan 162
03-3260-2750

Kato, Yoshiro
Motoko Ishii Lighting Design Inc.
Mil Design House, 5-4-11 Sendagaya
Shibuya-ku, Tokyo, Japan 151
03-3353-5311

Kaufman, Elliott
955 West 90th Street, #5C
New York, NY 10024
(212) 496-0860

Kohno, Yutaka
3-9-6-501 Minamisenba
Minami-ku, Osaka, Japan
06-245-5503

Korab, Balthazair
Helikon-Photo Ges.m.b.H
A-1070 Wien
Kircheng, 41 Austria
0222-96-67-03

Leibow, Alan
WGFS Lighting
5855 Green Valley Circle, #304
Culver City, CA 90230
(310) 216-1670

Lowry, Michael
Michael Lowry Photography
P.O. Box 681191
Orlando, FL 32868
(407) 291-1464

Lumen Architectural Photography
P.O. Box 09867
Columbus, OH 43209
(614) 237-5977

McGee, E. Alan
1816 Briarwood End Court
Atlanta, GA 30329
(404) 633-1286

McGrath, Norman
164 West 79th Street
New York, NY 10024
(212) 799-6422

Mooney, John David
John David Mooney Studio
114 West Kinzie Street
Chicago, IL 60610
(312) 822-0483

Peterson, Jon
Jon Peterson Photography, Inc.
628 East Third Avenue
Tulsa, OK 74120
(918) 585-2509

Quesada, Gary
P.O. Box 895
Troy, MI 48099-0895
(313) 641-8881

Sakai, Yutaka
1-4-1-201 Fujimidai
Kunitachi-shi, Tokyo, Japan 186
0425-74-7884

Salin, Douglas A.
647 Joost Avenue
San Francisco, CA 94127-2340
(415) 584-3322

Santiago, Elan
655 Sutter Street
San Francisco, CA 94105
(415) 274-2200

Schanuel, Tony
10901 Oasis Drive
St. Louis, MO 63123
(314) 849-3495

Segal, Mark
Mark Segal Photography
230 North Michigan Avenue, #3700
Chicago, IL 60601
(312) 236-8545

Steinkamp, James R.
Steinkamp/Ballogg Photography
311 North Desplaines, Suite 409
Chicago, IL 60661
(312) 902-1233

Vanderwarker, Peter
28 Prince Street
West Newton, MA 02165
(617) 964-2728

Whalen, Stephen
Stephen Whalen Photography
2120 Jimmy Durante Blvd., Suite U
Del Mar, CA 92014
(619) 755-3485

Yamazaki, Yoichi
Motoko Ishii Lighting Design Inc.
Mil Design House, 5-4-11 Sendagaya
Shibuya-ku, Tokyo, Japan 151
03-3353-5311

INDEX